THE POLITICS OF IDEAS IN
THE U.S.S.R.

THE CONTEMPORARY SOVIET UNION SERIES:
INSTITUTIONS AND POLICIES

Each volume in the Contemporary Soviet Union Series examines in detail the facts about an important aspect of Soviet rule as it has affected the Soviet citizen in the 50 years since the Bolshevik Revolution of 1917.

Subjects include industry, culture, religion, agriculture, and so on. A careful examination of official Soviet material in each field provides essential basic reading for all students of Soviet affairs.

Robert Conquest is a former Research Fellow in Soviet affairs at the London School of Economics and Political Science and Senior Fellow of Columbia University's Russian Institute. His works include *Power and Policy in the USSR, The Pasternak Affair: Courage of Genius, Common Sense About Russia, The Soviet Deportation of Nationalities,* and *Russia after Khrushchev.*

THE CONTEMPORARY SOVIET UNION SERIES:
INSTITUTIONS AND POLICIES
EDITED BY ROBERT CONQUEST

The Politics of Ideas
in the U.S.S.R.

FREDERICK A. PRAEGER, *Publishers*
New York · Washington

BOOKS THAT MATTER
Published in the United States of America in 1967
by Frederick A. Praeger, Inc., Publishers
111 Fourth Avenue, New York, N.Y. 10003

Introduction © Robert Conquest, 1967

Library of Congress Catalog Card Number: 67–27314

This book is Number 197 in the series
Praeger Publications in Russian History and World Communism

Printed in Great Britain

Contents

Editor's Preface

One of the salient characteristics of the Soviet style of rule is the concern of the political leadership with the regulation of the public expression of ideas. Nor is this a matter only of politics proper, but extends into the humanities and sciences, and even, within limits which vary from time to time, into literary work.

The Soviet position does not arise from Marxist principles as such. Marx himself spoke strongly against the censored Press. Indeed, he flatly countered the Soviet view-point when he wrote: 'The censored Press, a bad Press, remains bad, even when giving good products. A free Press remains good, even when giving bad products.'* And Lenin, when he seized power in 1917, at first permitted not only the Menshevik and other opposition Socialist Press, but even the newspapers of the 'bourgeois' Kadet party. The total suppression of opposition thought was not complete until about 1920.

Rosa Luxemburg, the Polish Communist theoretician and martyr who was killed in 1919, was critical of the Soviet régime even in those early days. Though herself in many ways on the left of the Communist movement, and a strong believer in the 'proletarian dictatorship', she continued to hold that freedom of speech and free elections were essentials for the healthy development of a socialist state. Nor did she define 'freedom' in some esoteric fashion to mean freedom simply to support the government. She said clearly enough, 'Freedom only for the supporters of the government, only for the members of one party—however numerous they may be—is no freedom at all. Freedom is always and exclusively freedom for the one who thinks differently.' She did not maintain this out of attachment to abstract principle, but because she saw that 'without unrestricted freedom of press and assembly, without a free

* Marx, *Collected Works*, MEGA Edition, Vol. I.

[7]

struggle of opinion, life dies out in every public institution.' She foresaw that the result would be that bureaucracy alone would remain the active element, and no more than 'a dozen' or so leaders would in fact control everything. She even had the acuteness to prophesy that 'such conditions must inevitably cause a brutalisation of public life: attempted assassinations, shooting of hostages, etc.'*

Rosa Luxemburg's essential point, that life would die out of the body politic, and all the energy of the free intellect and creative thinking would be replaced by the energies emanating from a small ruling group, may be regarded as in a sense the key to the whole of Soviet development.

It went far further than the imposition of consistent political dogma. Soviet Marxism, though in principle a scientific and 'science-orientated' doctrine, nowhere preserved the implied rationality. Vulgarised philosophical dogma was intruded into non-political fields of thought. Several pseudo-sciences have at various times been incorporated in the Communist canon: Lysenkoist biology, Marrist linguistics, Zhdanovite aesthetics, and Morganist anthropology. The most scandalous of these— Lysenkoism—prevailed until the fall of Khrushchev in 1964. That is, biological teaching depended on the vagaries of the political struggle.

On the other hand, it was Stalin himself who suddenly denounced and suppressed Marrism in 1950—accusing its adherents of having employed authoritarian methods in imposing their views. Such abrupt changes appear illogical from a strictly doctrinal point of view. But the essential is not doctrine but discipline. As Daniel Bell has put it, 'the central fact is not any specific theoretical formulation *but the basic demand for belief in the Party itself* ... it is not the creed but the insistence on the infallibility of the interpreters that becomes the necessary mechanism of social control.'† When Stalin was the sole qualified interpreter, this attitude led to the imposition on the world of learning of the merest whims of the tyrant. He happened, for example, to remark once in an aside that the Azerbaidzhani were obviously descended from the Medes. There is no basis for such a notion, nor, of course, was it of

* Rosa Luxemburg, *The Russian Revolution* (Ann Arbor, 1961).
† *Slavic Review*, December 1965, p. 602 (Professor Bell's italics).

[8]

any party significance. But it became a doctrine, and academic linguists even spent fifteen years trying to find Median words in Azeri; 'eventually thirty-five dubious Median words were found, though the Median language is itself mythical.'*

There are many such stories. It will be seen that in this period perversion of thought for merely arbitrary reasons, not truly connected with the Party's *raison d'état*, flourished. The end of this particular type of monstrosity came with the end of the 'personality cult'. But the more basic, if less extravagant, misunderstandings which served the Party or its corporate myths persisted and persist.

Even as to the determination of Marxist doctrine itself, the situation is not satisfactory. For the final decision rests, and has always rested, on the Central Committee of the Party, while no prominent Marxist scholar has succeeded in avoiding heresy. Party philosophers have always eventually fallen foul of the political authorities. The old Communist economists were almost all purged in 1929–30, most of them suffering physical extinction in the ensuing period. The Communist historians came under mounting attack, and during the great trials of the mid-thirties many of them were denounced by name as terrorists. It was even said that there was a special 'historical' group of plotters.†

For most striking of all has been the attitude not to opinion, but to historical fact. Under Stalin a great edifice of falsehood became the only tolerated type of recent history. Since the repudiation of Stalin's excesses, much of this has been abandoned. The myths of the Khrushchev period were less offensive; and many of these too have now gone. But there remain whole periods of which no true account is available to the Soviet citizen.

Stalin's false accusations against the opposition leaders shot in 1936–38 are not persisted with, but most of those then accused have not been publicly acquitted, and in effect no consistent version, true or false, now obtains. Again, in Stalin's time not only the old opposition leaders but many executed Stalinists disappeared from the history books; now, those

* All-Union Conference on Measures to Improve the Training of Scientific-pedagogical Cadres in the Historical Sciences, Moscow 1964, p. 338 (quoted below as *Vsesoyuznoe Soveshehanie Istorikov*).
† Radek's evidence at the January 1937 trial.

Stalinists have been rehabilitated but other names, such as Molotov's, have gone into oblivion. Soviet encyclopedias and reference books still omit entirely the names of at least four, and sometimes five, of the eight men who have been premiers of the Soviet Union—though they give the premiers of Tsarist times.

'The Politics of Ideas' is a convenient formulation for bringing under one head the various methods employed in the USSR to impose the current ideas of the Party and to suppress all others. It should not be taken as meaning that there are no areas in which autonomous thought can exist. In physics, for example, in spite of a certain amount of bullying by dogmatists suspicious of the philosophical implications of modern theory (and in spite of arrests, in the Stalin period, of many prominent physicists), a comparatively normal intellectual life continued. And even in more sensitive spheres like literature, where not only the political implications but even the artistic form is the constant concern of the cultural apparatchiks, a certain vagueness has always prevailed about the precise frontier between the permitted and the heretical. (Poetry, for example, is notoriously refractory to any sort of exact analysis, and this includes the ideological.) In this ill-defined penumbra a struggle has always taken place between the force of 'dogmatism' and of 'liberalism', the result for the moment depending on the general degree of rigour prevailing at the top political level. For, whatever the particular decision taken, it is there that the central initiative always resides.

Oscillation between rigour and relaxation has continued. In general, the past few years have seen notable improvements in the literary and scientific fields. In many areas open debates have taken place (though we should, indeed, recall that even in Stalin's time occasional controversies were permitted, such as that between Varga and Vosnesensky on important economic issues in 1948). On the debit side there is also much to note. The Sinyavsky-Daniel trial in February 1966 marked the imprisonment on political grounds of writers who had, in fiction of what would ordinarily be regarded as a non-political type, given offence to the authorities. In 1966 new laws were passed which included the fresh Article 190 of the Criminal Code, making it an offence to disseminate in oral or written form 'conscious fabrications discrediting the Soviet State'. As Soviet intellectuals pointed out, this left the interpretation of what should be regarded as 'fabrications' in the hands of the State and its judiciary.

For these and similar official acts roused many protests from some of the most distinguished scientists and writers of Russia. The Party cannot easily attack these leading figures, unless and until it is prepared to go to extreme lengths. But when it comes to young and little-known writers not defended by their long-established reputations, like the poets Batshev and Ginsburg, they are exiled, imprisoned or (in an old Russian tradition) confined to asylums whenever opportunity arises; and a number are so suffering as I write.

If the present atmosphere is nevertheless more promising than it has been, this is due almost entirely to such resistance by the intelligentsia to the full rigours of the Party's claims, rather than to any abatement of the latter in principle. It is not necessarily a stable situation. Early in 1963, after a similar period of 'thaw', a reaction set in which the accidents of the political struggle at the top fortunately rendered abortive; but at the time it was widely feared among Soviet writers that a period of terror against them was once again about to start.

It can scarcely be said that any truly 'liberal' trend has revealed itself in the political leadership. The attitudes might rather be said to vary between those who favour repression pure and simple, and those who are prepared to allow certain concessions. Nothing, in fact, is established on a permanent or reliable basis, and no legal or institutional guarantees can be said to exist. Moreover, even the freest debate is still held within the limits of full acceptance of the Party's right to rule as it does. It is quite unknown, for example, for any slightest suggestion that Lenin may have been wrong to appear. That is, a non-rational, mythological attitude to history and politics still essentially prevails.

In this book we document and detail the history and the nature of the Soviet system of 'thought-control', of the conscious limitation and guidance of permitted expression in every sphere.

Robert Conquest

Acknowledgements are due to Messrs. H. S. Murray, I. I. Stepanov, L. Levine and M. Friedman for their invaluable collaboration.

[11]

I

The Theory:
Historical Materialism, Ideology
and Determinism

Soviet Communists believe that man can be refashioned in a new image, since Communist society will be one in which

'the enslaving subordination of the individual to the division of labour, and therewith also the antithesis between mental and physical labour, has vanished ... labour has become not only a means of life but life's prime want ... the productive forces have also increased with the all-round development of the individual, and all the springs of co-operative wealth flow more abundantly—only then can ... society inscribe on its banners: From each according to his ability, to each according to his needs!'[1]

This vision, seen by Marx in 1875, implies a radical change in human nature. In 1917 Lenin referred to the foresight of 'the great Socialists' for whom Communism 'presupposed both a productivity of labour unlike the present and a person *unlike the present* man in the street ...'.[2]

How is this change to be brought about? Marxism gives a paradoxical answer. For the change in human nature is seen both as a consequence and as a condition of the alteration of the economic basis of society. On the one hand there is the original determinist tradition of Marx's historical materialism: on this showing, man is conditioned by his social environment and the new society will produce the new man as the old produced the old. On the other hand, as Lenin saw, the new society *presupposes* the new man, who must therefore, it would seem, be created artificially. The apparatus of Soviet education and thought control has this creation as its ultimate ostensible purpose. But the very existence of the apparatus has involved a substantial shift in Marxist theory for it implies that the Soviet leaders attribute great importance to the influence of ideas and ideology in the life of man.

The Marxist revolt against Rationalism involved a devaluation of ideas. In Marx's view, religious, political, legal, and other ideas, or (as he called them) 'forms of consciousness', were part of the 'superstructure' of society, which in turn was 'determined' by the 'base' consisting of economic relationships. In the words of the classic text, Marx's Preface to the *Critique of Political Economy*:

'The sum total of . . . production relations constitutes the economic structure of society, the real foundation on which a legal and political superstructure arises and to which definite forms of social consciousness correspond. The mode of production of material life conditions the social, political and spiritual life-process in general. It is not the consciousness of men that determines their being, but, on the contrary, their social being determines their consciousness.'[3]

All the makers of Marxist ideology have quoted or echoed this passage. 'What is known as the ideologies', wrote Plekhanov in 1897, 'is nothing but a multiform reflection in the minds of men of [a] single and indivisible history . . . the history of their own social relations, which are determined by the state of the productive forces at each given period.'[4] Lenin, in one of his earliest works, said that Marx's and Engels' 'basic idea' was just this division of social relationships into two types—material and ideological, the latter being 'merely a superstructure of the former'.[5] Stalin formulated it in 1938: '. . . the material life of society, its being, is also primary, and its spiritual life secondary, derivative . . .'.[6] The Party Programme adopted in 1961 shows how, under Khrushchev, it was argued that an abundance of material plenty heralded the arrival of Communism. A practical by-product was the winning of material primacy in the competition with capitalism, to the world's consequent admiration.[7] The thesis that it is not ideas but economic forces that are fundamental in history is deeply embedded in Marxist doctrine.

Nevertheless, from early on, it was plain that thus baldly stated, the proposition would not do. It was too easy to infer that ideology (including Marxism itself, presumably) was not only secondary, but unimportant. A rider was therefore introduced to correct such an impression, and it is in the development of this correction to the original statement that the shift in theory has occurred. The process began at least as early as 1890, when Engels wrote:

[14]

'The economic situation is the basis, but the various elements of the superstructure . . . also exercise their influence on the course of the historical struggles and in many cases preponderate in determining their *form*. There is an interaction of all these elements, in which . . . the economic movement finally asserts itself as necessary.'[8]

By 1902 Lenin had found that political activity involves the use of ideology. Too impatient to allow the Russian working-class movement to develop gradually on the basis of economic pressure, he was concerned to imbue it with revolutionary class-consciousness. This, he argued, could be brought to the working class only 'from outside'—that is, by non-proletarian intellectuals. 'Socialism is *introduced* by ideologists into the proletariat's class struggle which develops spontaneously on the basis of capitalist relationships.'[9] In the autumn of 1917, shortly before the Bolshevik seizure of power, Lenin was even more specific. In 1844, many years before he formulated the doctrine of historical materialism, Marx had written: 'material force must be overthrown by material force; but theory, too, becomes a material force as soon as it has gripped the masses.'[10] Part of this sentence is now echoed by Lenin:

'Ideas become a force when they get hold of the masses. And particularly now, when the Bolsheviks . . . have embodied in their policy the idea which moves the innumerable toiling masses in the whole world.'[11]

These remarks by Marx and Lenin, suggesting a definite positive rôle for ideas, were uttered under the impulse of a practical situation rather than as considered contributions to the theory of historical materialism. A more cautious statement by Bukharin in 1921 is more characteristic of official Marxist theory at this period. 'The theory of historical materialism' he wrote, 'does not deny the importance of the superstructure in general and of the ideologies in particular, but explains them . . . [which] is quite a different matter.'[12]

The real turning point—what might be called the rehabilitation of the superstructure—occurred when the Five-Year Plans were getting into their stride and when the State, under Stalin, not only showed no signs of 'withering away' as Engels had prophesied, but took control of every aspect of the life of its citizens. In these circumstances the theory had to be given a fresh twist to justify the omnipresent superstructure, which was plainly something more than a mere reflection of the underlying economic 'base'. Stalin produced the necessary reformulation in 1938:

'As regards the *significance* of social ideas, theories, views and political institutions, as regards their *rôle* in history, historical materialism, far from denying them, stresses the important rôle of these factors in the life of society, in its history,'[13]

He went on to distinguish between old social ideas which, 'hamper the development, the progress of society', and new 'advanced' ideas which 'facilitate the development, the progress of society' and have 'tremendous organising, mobilising, and transforming value'.

This latter description of the rôle of the superstructure—which Stalin repeated several times—represented a considerable departure from the original spirit of Marxism. It is not surprising that the only text from Marx which Stalin found to support it was the familiar *obiter dictum*: 'Theory becomes a material force as soon as it has gripped the masses.'

No less explicit and, from the classical Marxist point of view, no less extraordinary, were Stalin's remarks on the same subject during the Soviet linguistics controversy of 1950. Although, according to Stalin, the superstructure is 'generated' by the base, it then turns out to be a 'most active force which contributes vigorously to the formation and consolidation of its base, takes all steps to assist the new order to drive the old base and the former classes into the dust and liquidate them.'[14]

No significant revision of the theory of base and superstructure has taken place since these statements. Despite all the developments in other fields since Stalin's death, they continue to provide the basis for the official line on the subject.[15]

Closely associated with the rehabilitation of the superstructure in Soviet society was the introduction of a dynamic, purposive, driving attitude of mind—what might be called a Five-Year-Plan mentality—into many fields of life. Here, however, there was little or no need to revise basic tenets. From the first Marxism had contrived to combine a declared philosophical determinism with Marx's own aphorism that the philosophers 'have only *interpreted* the world in various ways; the point, however, is to *change* it'.[16] For clear manifestations of the change from a deterministic attitude to a purposive one, which took place in Soviet thinking about the end of the 1920s, we must look less at successive statements of Marxist doctrine than at developments in the various fields of intellectual life which were mobilised to serve the end of 'building Socialism' at that time.

SOURCES

1. Marx and Engels, Vol. II, p. 23.
2. Lenin, Vol. 25, p. 441.
3. Marx and Engels, Vol. I, p. 329; cf. Bukharin, p. 207.
4. Plekhanov, p. 43.
5. Lenin, Vol. I, pp. 133f.
6. Stalin, p. 724.
7. *Programma i Ustav KPSS*, pp. 112, 168.
8. Marx and Engels, Vol. II, p. 443.
9. Lenin, Vol. 6, p. 143.
10. Marx and Engels, *Sochineniya*, Vol. 1, p. 422.
11. Lenin, Vol. 26, p. 104.
12. Bukharin, p. 226.
13. Stalin, pp. 726f.
14. Stalin, *On Marxism in Linguistics*, quoted in Murra, p. 70.
15. Rozenthal and Yudin, p. 39; *Filosofskaya Entsiklopediya* (Philosophical Encyclopedia), State Scientific Publishing House 'Soviet Encyclopedia', Moscow, 1960, Vol. I, p. 124.
16. Marx and Engels, Vol. II, p. 367.

II

The Mobilisation
of Thought after 1928

Communist decisions to industrialise the Soviet Union and to collectivise its agriculture, taken in 1925 and 1927 respectively, implied a sweeping and indeed violent exercise of the power of the central authorities. The implementation of these decisions involved the most rigorous mobilisation not only of manpower and natural resources but of thought itself.

In economics, philosophy, psychology, education, literature, and history—to take only a selection—the period saw fundamental shifts in principle which are directly connected with the emergence of a totalitarian régime in the Soviet Union. Free speculative ideas were replaced by practical, applied thinking, harnessed to the needs of the State. Objectivity and the pursuit of truth for its own sake—so far as they had survived—gave place to partisanship, propaganda, and, ultimately, to falsification. In no case was the transition effected without direct intervention by party or State, and many scholars and artists suffered in the process.

ECONOMICS

Before the Revolution, Russian economists had included some figures of considerable distinction, particularly in business cycle theory. These thinkers, many of whom were influenced by Marxist ideas, saw it as their task to do what Marx had claimed to do but never did—to study the economy objectively and to try to discern economic laws of general validity. Elements of this tradition, and some of its exponents, survived in the Soviet Union for some years after the Revolution. As the State began to exercise more and more pressure, however, this type of objectivity became gradually more reprehensible. The concept of 'economic law' itself was removed from the Soviet economist's field of vision, until, many years later, it reappeared out of the mouth of Stalin.

In the mid-1920s three attitudes were discernible among Soviet economists towards economic law, two extreme and one intermediate. The background was the mixed nature of the New Economic Policy (NEP), part nationalised and part in private hands. On the one hand Professor N. D. Kondratyev, a pre-revolutionary economist of note who, in 1920, became head of the Institute for Market Forecasting (*Konyunkturny Institut*) attached to the Timiryazev Agricultural Academy,[1] saw economic law as a factor severely limiting the scope of planning. The intermediate view was represented by E. A. Preobrazhensky, who considered the NEP economy as an arena for a 'struggle between two laws . . . the law of primary Socialist accumulation [in the planned sector] and the law of value [in the private sector].'[2]

The law of Socialist accumulation, according to Preobrazhensky, was none other than the first stage, the 'childhood', of the planning principle. The real struggle was between the planning principle and the law of value.[3] The other extreme was exemplified by two economists, A. Leontyev and E. Khmelnitskaya, who admitted no 'law' at all in the planned sector of the economy:

'The struggle is a struggle for the elimination and destruction of *all* economic laws . . . and for the replacement of these laws by the regularities of organised economy, recognised by social man, who acts as the medium for their operation.'[4]

But, according to Leontyev and Khmelnitskaya, economic necessity (determinism) remains—only it 'finds realisation more and more in the economic policy of the proletarian dictatorship'.[5]

These arguments, which may seem to be disputes about words (what is a 'law' and what a 'regularity'?) were the theoretical aspect of a more practical dispute about the function of planning. Kondratyev defined the rôle of planning as being to

'avoid the fetish of exact calculations; . . . it must bow before an understanding of those processes which are in actual motion in the economy; we must grasp the basic processes that confront us.'[6]

Two senior economists in *Gosplan*, V. A. Bazarov and V. G. Groman, agreed broadly with Kondratyev. Bazarov described his theory of planning as 'genetic' as opposed to 'teleological', meaning that it should grow out of the past rather than direct the future. Groman evolved a constant exchange ratio between industry and agriculture, which, in his view, would dominate and limit other elements in the plan.[7] The opposing view was stated by another eminent Soviet economist, S. G. Strumilin, who wrote: 'The art of planning does not reconcile itself to the existing world. Its aim is not to know this world, but to change it. It creates a new world for itself, actively.'[8]

Behind this controversy lay yet another, still more practical. How fast could industrialisation proceed? The party and economists like Strumilin tended to be optimistic; Kondratyev and his fellow-thinkers to be cautious. In the event, the party intervened to settle the issue in favour of optimism. In 1927 a resolution of the Central Committee called for a radical change in the character of the Control Figures (as the annual plan was then called) so that they should offer 'not only general guidance, but also concrete directives and limits for drawing up all operative plans and the State Budget'.[9] The previous control figures, it was later stated, incorporated the 'anti-party understanding of the Plan as "prognosis",' instead of the 'Lenin-Stalin understanding of the Plan as directives . . . aimed at the revolutionary transformation of the country'.[10] This is contrasted with the control figures of later years, which 'were compiled on the basis of special party directives. . . . From 1927–28 Plan onwards, the control figures . . . . became a most important instrument of Socialist construction'.[11]

It was not long before the 'genetically-minded' economists felt the weight of party disapproval. In 1929 Groman, head of the Market Forecasting Council of *Gosplan*, a member of the Presidium of *Gosplan* and of the Collegium of the Central Statistical Administration, who had been to Geneva with the Soviet delegation in 1927 and had been awarded the title of Honoured Worker in Science the same year, was dismissed from his posts. In September, 1930, 'when the anti-Soviet nature of his activity was finally disclosed', he was arrested, with 'other economists of Menshevik and *kulak* ideology'.[12] The other economists included Kondratyev and Bazarov, Chayanov (a well-known agricultural expert), and Yurovsky (a financial specialist). All were accused of a plot to undermine the Five-Year Plan and the Soviet economy, but only Groman, who had a Menshevik background, was brought to public trial. He was sentenced to 10 years' imprisonment in 1931. Remarkably, only Bazarov appears to have died in the purge. The others were listed as still being alive in 1957.[13]

However, the disappearance from public life of the men associated with the idea of planning as 'prognosis' was heavy with implications for economics in the Soviet Union. It involved the loss of an entire attitude of mind. The objective, detached viewpoint, regarding society as a developed organism to be studied scientifically—the very attitude which Marx had claimed for himself—was henceforward condemned. Economics was identified with Marxism-Leninism, based openly on the 'class interests of the proletariat'.[14] Economic theory was subordinated to practical considerations,[15] which meant, in effect, that it was wholly neglected. No general textbook on economics was published between 1928 and 1954. The Soviet economist lost his independence and became part of the mechanism of the State.

PHILOSOPHY

Karl Marx was a student of philosophy before he was a Communist, and Communism has always been distinguished among revolutionary movements by the emphasis it lays on its philosophy—that is, on dialectical materialism. Since 1922, when Berdyaev and other 'idealist' philosophers who had organised a 'Free Religio-Philosophical Academy' after the Revolution were expelled from the country,[16] dialectical materialism has been the only philosophy taught in the Soviet Union.

Nevertheless, even within these limits, there has been scope for controversy and heresy. The first few years after the Revolution saw the rise of a crude biological materialism preached by E. S. Enchman and some other Communists, which sought to abolish philosophy, including dialectical materialism, altogether.[17] This trend, which embodied a literal-minded interpretation of the Marxist claim to be 'scientific', died out, largely under Bukharin's criticisms, about 1924. But the emphasis on the empirical sciences, on which it had been based, produced the Soviet philosophical heresy known as 'mechanism'.

The controversy between the 'mechanists' and the 'dialecticians' lasted from about 1925 to 1929. Philosophical mechanism was, in fact, a variant of the detached and objective attitude of mind which, as became abundantly clear towards the end of the 1920s, was incompatible with Soviet Communism. The leaders of the mechanist school, Professor A. K. Timiryazev, a physicist, Professor V. Sarabyanov, an economist, and I. I. Skvortsov-Stepanov, an erudite Marxist, translator of *Das*

Kapital, and writer on scientific subjects, held that the complex laws governing the behaviour of living matter, including man and society, could be reduced to the simpler physio-chemical laws, and that these in turn could be reduced to the simplest laws of mechanical movement.

The dialecticians, led by A. M. Deborin, introduced a more dynamic principle, basing themselves on Engels' *Dialectics of Nature,*[18] which had been published only in 1925. They held that motion was an immanent attribute of matter, and to say that the laws of living matter could be reduced to simple mechanical laws was thus incorrect. Among those whom the dialecticians accused of mechanism was Bukharin because of his partiality for the concept of equilibrium. Equilibrium, they argued, knows only motion and rest, which are quite different from the 'immanent movement' in their own scheme of things. The dialecticians found a connection between Bukharin's philosophical views and his distrust of the Party's policy of forced industrialisation and the 'liquidation of the *kulaks* as a class'.[19]

The battle between the two groups was joined at a conference of Marxist-Leninist Scientific Institutions in April, 1929— the month in which Bukharin was stripped of most of his political power. The result was, therefore, a foregone conclusion. The conference passed a resolution condemning the mechanists' views, stating that the 'theoretical discussion with the mechanists is really finished'.[20]

At this point the Communist Party intervened overtly by instructing the Communist Academy—which was a Party body —to see that the dialectical point of view was introduced in the Natural Sciences, including psychology.[21] This, however, was only a beginning. In December, 1929, Stalin, addressing the conference of Agrarian Marxists, said that

'theoretical thought is not keeping pace with our practical successes, that there is a certain gap between our practical successes and the development of theoretical thought. Yet our theoretical work must not only keep pace with practical work but must keep ahead of it and equip our practical workers for their fight for the victory of Socialism.'[22]

Stalin was referring explicitly to theoretical work in economics (in which the leading theorists had just been arrested) and agriculture. However, the philosophers were not slow to draw conclusions. As Julius Hecker, then a teacher of philo-

sophy in Moscow, and a consistent and informed apologist of
the party line, put it:

'Encouraged by these observations of Stalin, the Communist Party
organisation of the philosophical section of the Institute of Red
Professors called attention to the necessity for a radical change "on
the philosophical front".'[23]

The first sign that there was more to come in philosophy was
an article in *Pravda* of June 7, 1930, signed by M. Mitin, V.
Raltsevich, and P. Yudin. Deborin, the hero of the battle against
mechanism, was now found to be at fault. There were, it
seemed, two trends in Soviet philosophy—Marxism-Leninism
and Plekhanov-Menshevik idealism. Deborin and his school had
fallen into the latter heresy by failing to grasp 'Lenin's idea of
partisan (*partiiny*) philosophy'. Hecker continues his somewhat
ingenuous account:

'A very important fact in connection with the publication of this
article was the editorial support of *Pravda* for the arguments of the
authors. This fact made it more than the opinion of the authors, it
became the voice of the official organ of the Communist Party. . . .
Therewith [the controversy] became an issue between an important
party authority and the old philosophical leadership in the Communist Academy.'[24]

After a statement in self-defence by Deborin, the bureau of
the party cell of the Institute of Red Professors issued a resolution in *Pravda* on August 2, 1930. The main emphasis was laid
upon the failure of Soviet philosophers to keep up with the
'tasks of Socialist construction' and to maintain a closer connection with the life and the party struggle.

'The basic task in the near future must be the mobilisation of the
attention of the whole philosophical *aktiv* to questions of a decisive
turn of all theoretical work towards a study of problems of Socialist
construction.'[25]

Philosophers should defend the 'general line' of the party.
There was a particular need to train new 'theoretical cadres . . .
capable of satisfying the needs of modern tempos of Socialist
construction'. These cadres, moreover, should, in the first instance, be drawn from among proletarians, or from among those
who 'have experience of the Civil War . . . [and] have shown
their steadiness in the struggle against all anti-Leninist deviations'. The study of theory should be 'actualised . . . bringing it
nearer to the immediate tasks of Socialist construction'.[26]

[23]

Matters came to a head at an All-Union conference of philosophers in October, 1930. Before the conference, the Party organisation of the Institute of Red Professors adopted another resolution embodying a general indictment of the Deborin school. In this, socio-political demands on philosophy were frankly stated. The 'broad offensive of Socialism', the 'intensification of the class struggle', the 'elimination of the *kulaks* as a class'—these were the factors which, according to the Party group, necessitated a change in philosophy. The greatest fault of Deborin's group, it said, was their failure to grasp the importance of Lenin as a philosopher and their over-valuation of Plekhanov in this field. They even flirted with Trotskyism.[27]

Against this, Mitin's and Yudin's group put forward a programme for philosophy which emphasised its practical application to social problems. Dialectical materialism, they said, should become a 'philosophical science' applied to the techniques of natural science and 'the daily practice of Socialist construction and the class struggle'. Soviet philosophers should 'aid fraternal Communist Parties in their theoretical work'. They should continue the struggle against mechanism and also against the 'methodology of the Right-opportunist trend in the Communist Party', and should give a 'philosophic defence of the general policy of the Communist Party, particularly in its struggle with opportunist tendencies'.[28]

At the conference, according to Hecker's account, Deborin and his supporters were 'isolated from the outset', and his 'desperate attempt' to sway the conference towards his point of view met with no success. Mitin, who had become the main spokesman for the Institute of Red Professors' group, reiterated the charge that Deborin was transforming philosophy into a 'set of ideas altogether separate from the complete historical social class situation . . .'—a feature attributed to Deborin's 'Menshevising idealism'. By the end of the conference, which lasted three days, Deborin

'realised his defeat, and . . . changed his attitude and publicly confessed his former Menshevik errors. He also conceded that his group had taken a wrong attitude towards the party, and requested that his defence should be considered null and void.'[29]

The victors lost no time in making their position secure. At the end of 1930 the bureau of the party organisation of the Institute of Red Professors 'had a chat with Comrade Stalin'.[30]

This resulted, in January, 1931, in a resolution of the Central Committee of the Party by which Mitin and Yudin were appointed to the editorial board of the periodical *Under the Banner of Marxism*. Deborin remained an editor, but the resolution declared that the periodical

'must be a militant organ of Marxism-Leninism, and wage a decisive struggle for the general line of the Party and against all deviations from it, implementing consistently in all its work the Leninist principle of the Party-content of philosophy.'[31]

The resolution then explained what this meant in practice.

'In philosophy the periodical must wage an undeviating struggle on two fronts: against the mechanistic revision of Marxism . . . and also against the idealistic distinction of Marxism by Deborin . . . and others.'[32]

Deborin was thus set the task of demolishing the views he had professed until a few months previously; and he lost his position in the Philosophy Department of the Communist Academy.[33] His adaptability and readiness to eat his words, however, saved him from extinction and he held posts of diminishing importance until he died in 1963. Mitin and Yudin have, on the other hand, gone from strength to strength. Both are Academicians and former editors of the *Large Soviet Encyclopedia*, and from 1956–1961 they were full members of the Party Central Committee. Mitin has held various posts in the All-Union Society for the Dissemination of Political and Scientific Knowledge (now known as the *Znanie* Society) and in early 1966 was still chief editor of the periodical *Questions of Philosophy*. Yudin was Soviet Ambassador in China from 1953 to October 1959. In the hands of men such as these philosophy in the Soviet Union has finally and firmly been harnessed to the Party machine. 'The Central Committee of the Party' as Yudin put it in 1931, '[is] the theoretical centre of Marxism-Leninism'.[34]

PSYCHOLOGY

The first effect of the Revolution on Russian psychology was to drive out the 'subjectivist' or 'introspectionist' psychologists such as Lossky and Frank, who had been widely esteemed before 1917. Initially, however, the drive against the subjectivists was based not on Marxism but on natural science. Its leaders were Ivan Pavlov, the physiologist, and V. N. Bekhterev, who adopted the desciption of 'reflexologist'. These two scholars tended to reduce all human behaviour to biological reflexes and to deny the value of psychology altogether.[35]

The impact of Marxism was rather to offset this narrowly biological approach. In 1922, K. N. Kornilov undertook the defence of psychology as a science, stating that it should be based on dialectical materialism.[36] He gained influence and in 1923 became head of the Moscow State Institute of Experimental Psychology, in place of Chelpanov.[37] But until about 1930, psychology had to struggle to exist against 'reflexology', which gained from a kinship with physiology, and hence from the immense prestige of Pavlov himself.

Marxism, in Kornilov's view, should lend psychology three principles—the materialist, the determinist, and the dialectical.[38] Although he supported psychology as a science, these principles meant that the difference between him and the anti-psychological schools of Pavlov and Bekhterev was often reduced to hair-splitting. Kornilov for instance, brought his views into line with materialism by saying that the *psyche* 'is not something opposed to matter, but only an *aspect of the most highly organised form of matter*'.[39] Like the reflexologists, he denied that psychic phenomena could form part of a casual chain independent of physical phenomena.[40]

The model of human personality that emerged was that of a mechanism, or a set of inter-related reactions to external forces. Man was regarded as a relatively passive, adaptive creature, largely incapable of controlling his behaviour. The most that he could do was to react in such a way as to maintain a state of equilibrium with environment.[41] But although all accepted this model, there was still room for dispute on the problem of heredity *versus* environment since these two factors determine human behaviour. The biological influence on Soviet psychology here tended to weigh in favour of heredity, and this could be represented as a necessary corollary of 'materialism'.[42]

Marxism, however, coupled with the Soviet intention to create a 'new type of man', spoke for environment and the plasticity of the human personality. The theme of plasticity was particularly emphasised by A. B. Zalkind, a psychologist attached in succession to two Party bodies—the Institute of Communist Education and the Materialist Psycho-neurologists of the Communist Academy.[43] There was never any doubt that the authorities favoured the environmentalist view. The fact that intelligence testing or other investigations showed undesirable qualities in Soviet citizens, which then had to be explained by faults in social environment, was at this period no bar to the environmental interpretation as environment was seen largely as a remnant of the old régime. By the end of the 1920s the primacy of the social environment in determining behaviour was accepted, at least *pro forma*, even by the reflexologists.[44]

Both the biological and social explanations rested on deterministic assumptions. Man was passive: his own consciousness counted for little. 'During the entire period [of the 1920s] ...', a Soviet authority has written, the 'subject-matter of psychology was the behaviour of man, not his *psyche*, and not his consciousness'.[45] Will-power was discounted. A. R. Luriya wrote:

> 'Many observations support our view that the consideration of the voluntary act as accomplished by "will-power" is a myth, and that the human [being] cannot by direct force control his behaviour any more than a "shadow can carry stones".'[46]

With rare exceptions, Soviet psychologists of the 1920s dismissed the conscious factor.[*]

This approach, however conveniently it might accord with Marxist texts, proved to be seriously out of tune with the Party's policy of forced industrialisation. Psychology began to be affected by the new policy about November, 1928, when the leadership of the Moscow Society of Neuro-pathologists and Psychiatrists was swept away and replaced by a 'Marxist cadre' which, it is said, 'brought a broad scientific and practical democratisation to the society, and guaranteed a further Marxist formulation of the basic activities of Soviet psycho-neurologists'.[49] In April, 1929, the Materialist Psycho-neurologists of the Communist Academy—an organ of the Party Central Committee—took their cue from the dialecticians' victory in the current philosophical controversy and announced that in January, 1930, they would convene the First All-Union Congress for

---

[*] It was for this reason that many contemporary Soviet psychologists accepted the concept of the unconscious mind, because it reduces the rôle of conscious processes and thereby argues for the determinate nature of behaviour. Some elements of Freud's work, which was later to be rejected with odium, were popular at this time precisely because of his emphasis on the unconscious. 'Freud's psychic pan-determinism,' wrote Zalkind, 'is the best antidote to the entire doctrine of free will.'[47] The Freudian view of the unconscious and the subconscious is strongly rejected today.[48]

[27]

the Study of Human Behaviour. The congress was to be a step towards the introduction of dialectics into all the societies concerned with the subject.[50]

The 1930 congress marked the beginning of a new era, and a new orthodoxy, in Soviet psychology. During the decade that followed, the various trends of psychological thought, which had competed hitherto, were replaced by a single creed substantially different from all of them. The general lines were laid down at the congress itself, though it was some years before they were fully elaborated.

The principles of materialism and determinism were maintained in name, but largely discarded in substance. Psychic phenomena were now accorded their own order of causality. 'For Marxist psychology', it was declared 'it is . . . unacceptable to reduce psychic processes to . . . the conception of "reaction" or "reflex". . .'[51]

Psychology was thus assured the status of an autonomous discipline. By implication, it could be required to supply the basis for influencing the psychic elements in man—or, more plainly, for training the 'new man' required by the Soviet State. The next criticism of existing Soviet psychology was that it was 'based on the theory of equilibrium and ignored completely the problem of autogenetic movement'.[52] 'Autogenetic movement' meant that each system of matter or events moved itself, without extrinsic impulse. In psychology, this meant that a man's activity should be treated as something more than a series of reactions to environment. It restored to him the power of initiative.

This new emphasis meant that more attention could be given to training. In this connection Zalkind—incidentally putting the theoretical changes quite frankly in their social and political perspectives—renounced his previous Freudianism at the First Congress on Human Behaviour.

'How can we use the Freudian conception of man for Socialist construction? We need a socially "open" man who is easily collectivised and quickly and profoundly transformed in behaviour—a man capable of being a steady, conscious and independent person, politically and ideologically well trained.'[53]

Zalkind then asked: 'Does the "Freudian man" meet the demands of the task of Socialist construction?' He concluded that he did not, because the 'consciousness of this man is subordinated to the unconscious . . .'.[54]

[28]

At this stage Soviet psychology postulated not two, but three, factors determining behaviour—heredity, environment, and training. But as time went on, it became less and less acceptable politically to attribute such undesirable phenomena as delinquency or low-intelligence-test scores to social environment. A psychologist named Petrov, who investigated the intelligence of Chuvash children concluded, unfortunately, that their retarded state was due to inferior environment. This statement, harmless enough in the 1920s, led, in 1931, to a charge of counter-revolutionary thinking.[55]

In future the responsibility for failure would lie with the training of such children, *i.e.* with their teachers and family. Since the blame could thus be thrown on individuals rather than on the system, the process fell neatly within the limits of 'Bolshevik self-criticism'.

These shifts in emphasis were sharply accelerated by the Central Committee's decree 'On Pedological Perversions in the System of the People's Commissariats of Education', issued in July, 1936. This censured the Commissariat for undermining the position of the teacher by handing over to the pedologists (child psychologists) the most important functions of the school. The decree accused pedologists of believing that the 'fate of children is fatalistically conditioned by biological and social factors, the influence of heredity and of some kind of invariable environment'.[56] In fact, it added little in principle to the idea of psychology which had enjoyed official favour since the early 1930s. Significantly, the decree contained repeated complaints of the persistence of practices and ideas which had 'long been censured by the Party'.[57]

Its importance lay rather in the fact that it emerged from the Central Committee and that it attacked one specific group. This ensured that the ideas it embodied would be enforced. 'Cadres decide everything', Stalin had said in 1935.[58] The implications of this remark now became clear. Everything in psychology that was irrelevant to the training of Soviet citizens in the required image was to be cast aside.

To facilitate the task, however, one more theoretical step was taken after the decree against pedology. Heredity, environment, and training were found inadequate as factors determining behaviour. But the theory still allowed the pupil himself to blame conditions outside his control. To counter this, a fourth factor—self-training—was added. The psychologist Rubinshtein wrote in 1946: 'A man takes part in the shaping of his own character and he himself bears a responsibility for that character.'[59]

Soviet psychology, surviving the attacks of reflexology and physiology in the 1920s, won its scientific autonomy only to lose its political independence. Theoretical and experimental work suffered severely. By 1934 there were no specifically psychological periodicals published in the USSR, a position which remained unremedied until 1955.[60] Interesting experimental work, such as the study of pairs of identical twins, was stopped after 1936.[61] Psychology became an applied science, an ancillary arm of State policy.

EDUCATION

In education, as in other fields, the mobilisation of thought was reflected in sweeping changes in the early 1930s when the relatively untrammelled experimental ideas of the first years after the Revolution gave place to the practical, purposive criteria of the Five-Year Plans. Here it need only be pointed out that the shift in Soviet educational thought ran parallel to those in other disciplines—from determinism to activism, from idealism to realism, from the hopes raised by progressive theory to the realities of social demand.

Soviet schools during this period ceased to be a medium trying to provide an ideal environment in which the adolescent personality could blossom in a free self-governing community. Instead they became institutions designed to turn out loyal and productive Soviet citizens.

LITERATURE

The Communist view is that literature can only be tendentious and propagandist, at least while the class struggle lasts. This idea is found in the most important of Lenin's few statements on literary matters, his article *Party Organisation and Party Literature*, written in 1905. In it he proclaimed the principle of 'party literature' (*partiinaya literatura*). This meant not only that literature should not be a matter of money-making for individuals or groups, but that

'it cannot be an individual matter at all, independent of the common proletarian cause. Down with non-party *littérateurs*! Down with super-men *littérateurs*! Literature must become a *part* of the general proletarian cause, a "cogwheel" in a single great social-democratic mechanism, which is set in motion by the whole conscious *avant-garde* of the working class.'[62]

The bourgeois idea of freedom for the artist, according to Lenin, was illusory—'only a camouflaged dependence on the money-bag'. What had to be done was 'to substitute for a literature which is hypocritically free, but in fact bound to the bourgeoisie, a literature that is really free and *openly* bound to the proletariat'.[63]

From these statements, which became basic Soviet doctrine on literary matters, two consequences, one theoretical and one practical, flowed. The first was a theory of literature that emphasised its affective rather than its cognitive function. Literature should aim at influencing persons rather than at revealing truth. The second was that the Communist Party should be guide and controller in this field as much as anywhere else.

It was, however, some time after the Revolution before these consequences were realised. On the theoretical side, the leading Soviet literary critic of the 1920s, Voronsky, derived his ideas from Plekhanov rather than Lenin, and held that propaganda literature, useful in the Civil War period, was no longer enough. Literature should now reflect more truly the revolutionary reality.[64] 'Primarily,' he wrote, 'art is cognition of life.'[65] Voronsky did not deny the oft-quoted statement of Marx that the 'dominant ideas of any epoch are those of its dominant class', nor the deduction from this that literature should express a class psychology.[66] But he insisted that 'for the definition of art, the class concept is inadequate'.[67] Apart from the sociological analysis, Voronsky held that the critic should also evaluate a work aesthetically—that is, to '... determine to what extent its content ... is faithful to objective artistic truth'.[68]

These ideas led Voronsky to support literary trends such as the 'Serapion Brothers' and other unorthodox writers. He promptly ran into conflict, however, with the 'proletarian writers', grouped at this time round the magazine *On Guard*, which first appeared in June, 1923. This journal had a literary theory very different from Voronsky's:

'In a class society, fiction, just as everything else, serves the objects of a specific class, and, only through that class, of the whole of mankind; hence that literature is proletarian which organises the psychology and consciousness of the working class and of the toiling masses towards the final aims of the proletariat as the reorganiser of the world and the creator of Communist society. . . .

Proletarian literature opposes itself to bourgeois literature. . . . **We must stand firmly** *on guard over a strong and clear Communist ideology in proletarian literature.*'[69]

The *On Guard* group, in conformity with their view of literature, demanded party support.' Proletarian literature', they held, '[should] obtain the leading influence in the basic literary organs of the party and the Soviet Press.'[70]

In this they were to be largely disappointed. Hitherto the party had generally refrained from direct interference in literary politics.* In the current controversy, the party leaders were divided. Trotsky, Lunacharsky, and Ryazanov supported Voronsky, while Kamenev, Radek, and Yaroslavsky backed the proletarians.[72] It was not until 1925 that the party pronounced officially; and, when it did so, it offered a compromise solution.

The Central Committee declared on June 18, 1925, that the class war had not ended on the literary front, and that neutral art was impossible.[73] The party must 'secure the services of specialists and of all kinds of intellectuals and win them over ideologically from the bourgeoisie',[74] Sooner or later it must 'conquer positions in the field of fiction writing'.[75] Of the various groups of writers, the proletarians were relatively favoured. The party was to 'aid their development and in every way to support their organisations', although it must prevent the appearance of 'Communist conceit'.[76]

Peasant writers were to have 'full support', and the party was to 'guide their growing cadres on to the rails of proletarian ideology . . .'.[77] Generally, however, the resolution was remarkable for its restraint and liberality. Fellow-travellers, it said, required a 'tactful and careful' approach, and a 'patient attitude' which would help them 'to develop in the process of ever-closer comradely co-operation with the cultural forces of Commun-

* There is one notable exception. The *Proletcult*—the early organisation of proletarian writers which preached a distinct 'proletarian culture' and tried to remain independent of party and government—quickly incurred Lenin's displeasure and contempt. Regarding 'proletarian culture' as an artificial invention of bourgeois intellectuals and holding that Marxism did not reject 'the most valuable achievements of the bourgeois epoch, but, on the contrary, assimilated and re-worked all that was of value in the development of human thought and culture which has been going on for more than 2,000 years', Lenin forced the *Proletcult* to pass a resolution subordinating itself to the People's Commissariat of Education.[71]

ism'.[78] 'Tact, attention, and patience' should be shown towards any group which might 'join the proletariat',[79] and there should be 'free competition of various groups and tendencies', with no monopoly for any, 'even the one most proletarian in its ideological content'.[80] There should be no 'official, bureaucratic pseudo-solution' and no 'amateurish incompetent administrative interference in literary affairs'.[81]

These principles of party literary policy fell far short of what the proletarian writers demanded. The NEP period as a whole, from early 1921 to 1928, was marked by the same sort of relaxation in literature as in the economic field. This meant that there was a certain tolerance of non-Communist and non-committed writers, who, provided that their works could not be construed as counter-revolutionary, were able to get them published. Indeed, at this time, many Communist leaders looked upon them in the same way as they regarded non-Communist bourgeois experts in the economic and technological fields—as specialists whose superior knowledge and ability made them indispensable.

Not unnaturally, most writers, Communist and non-Communist alike, chose as the background for their works either the Revolution and the period of the Civil War or, looking to the future, the subject of material reconstruction. The first of a series of 'industrial' novels may thus have arisen spontaneously from genuine preoccupation. Examples are Gladkov's *Cement*, published in 1925, which may be considered their prototype, Vsevolod Ivanov's *Northsteel*, which appeared the same year, and Marietta Shaginyan's *Red Cottonreel*, published in 1926. But, in the context of thought control, it is perhaps necessary to draw a distinction between such 'industrial' novels, usually voluntarily and spontaneously executed (although they naturally elicited official encouragement and approval) and the 'Five-Year Plan' novels of the post-1928 period. These were largely the products of attempts to write to official dictation. Nor did the 'industrial' novels constitute anything but a relatively minor trend during the NEP period, the striking feature of which was the richness and variety of its literary production. It was mainly after 1928 that the enlistment of literature to serve the aims of material and economic progress placed a premium on mediocrity.

By that time the party had thought twice about its unwillingness to give the proletarian writers exclusive support. At an All-

3—P.O.I. [33]

Union Congress of Proletarian Writers in April of that year, Lunacharsky and two other important party officials spoke. Lunacharsky, who had previously supported Voronsky, said that the proletarian writers' chief virtue was their '100 per cent willingness' to carry out party directives. At the same time he now found it possible to justify his support for RAPP (the All-Union Proletarian Writers Organisation) on the ground that it 'includes a number of young people of outstanding talent—people who, in spite of the fact that they are overloaded with party tasks, are always working and studying'.[82] From now on RAPP became the party's watchdog in literary matters. In 1929 RAPP was said in *Pravda* to be following the line 'closest to the line of the party'.[83]

At the same time the party moved decisively away from the relatively tolerant policy towards literature that it had proclaimed in 1925. In December, 1928, the Central Committee ordered a general directive to be sent to publishing houses, placing emphasis on writings of a 'socially useful character' in all branches of publishing, including fiction. The party prescription for mass-circulation books included the following:

The publication of fiction is to be increased, especially of works on present-day themes and directed against bourgeois influences, philistinism, decadence, etc.

Mass-circulation books must be intelligible and accessible.

Such books must be an instrument for the mobilisation of the workers for the tasks of industrialisation and collectivisation.

Publishers should depend for the most part on Communist authors.[84]

Soon afterwards the Central Committee, through the medium of *Pravda* (with *Izvestiya* following suit), began to offer regular guidance to writers. The first editorial proclaimed that the literary page should be a 'sharp weapon' in the battle for Socialist culture, and it also called for 'more proletarian vigilance' and 'more Party leadership'.[85] Another editorial said:

'We must educate a type of literary man who can ... give a vital, gripping description of our Socialist construction, of all its gigantic achievements, and of all its failings. We need a fighting literature on contemporary themes, one that will react to the burning questions of Socialist construction and will daily mobilise the masses for the task of carrying out the general line of the party.'[86]

A Central Committee resolution 'On Publishing Work' in August, 1931, laid down what was generally expected of books:

[34]

'The content and character of a book should in every way respond to the demands of Socialist construction; it should be militant and deal with political themes of the present day; it should arm the broad masses of the builders of Socialism with Marxist-Leninist theory and with technical knowledge. Books should be the mightiest means of educating, mobilising and organising the masses for the tasks of economic and cultural construction.'[87]

Fiction writing, 'which plays an enormous educational rôle', was not forgotten in this almost military plan of campaign. It was to 'reflect far more *deeply and fully* the heroism of Socialist construction, the transformation of social relations and the growth of new people—the heroes of Socialist construction'.[88]

Apart from these general directives, the Party also sponsored various projects. Leonid Leonov and other prominent writers went to Turkestan, and Pilnyak to Central Asia, on 'missions' assigned by *Izvestiya*.[89] Gorky was made editor of a new magazine entitled *Our Achievements* (*Nashi Dostizheniya*) devoted entirely to sketches of 'Socialist construction', and a series of works called 'The History of Factories' (*Istoriya Zavodov*) was started with Gorky, Averbakh, Bukharin, and others on the editorial board.

Lastly, the 16th Party Conference initiated the publicisation of the names of the 'heroes of Socialist construction'.[90] *Pravda* duly elucidated:

'Have all the levers in the hands of the proletarian State been used; have all the newspapers, magazines, works of fiction, the films, the theatre, etc., been used for the portrayal of positive models of the militant initiative and enthusiasm of the millions? . . . We have before us the task of taking advantages of the most powerful levers for influencing the masses . . . for the portrayal of positive models of labour, for the portrayal of heroes and creators.'[91]

Literary men were enlisted, sometimes in 'Writers' Shock Brigades', for the most utilitarian purposes—for campaigns against drunkenness, against illiteracy, against wrecking, for the completion of spring sowing in a particular area. They were urged to observe, take part in, and describe the construction of 'industrial giants'.[92] Kaganovich, then a member of the Politburo of the Central Committee, summed up the Party proddings of literary men in the slogan: 'What we need is a *Magnitostroi* of literature.'[93]

The four years of RAPP's domination had their effect on the remaining non-Communist writers. Zamyatin was exceptionally fortunate in being allowed to leave the country. Even such an individualist as Pilnyak, whose novel *A Bare Year* (1922) had given a stark picture of life under 'War Communism', felt prompted to experiment in the new field and to re-write his novel *Mahogany* (1928) to the Five-Year Plan tune as *The Volga Falls into The Caspian Sea* (1930). Some, like Fedin and Kaverin, fell temporarily silent. Others adapted themselves. Marietta Shaginyan's *Hydrocentral* (1930–31), Leonov's *Sot* (1930) and *Skutarevsky* (1932), Velantin Kataev's *Forward, O Time!* (1932) were all Five-Year Plan novels written by non-Communists.

By 1932 the party was ready to undertake a further 'streamlining' of Soviet literature. In June, 1931, Stalin announced a change of policy towards the bourgeois 'specialists' employed in the Soviet economy. Wrecking, he said, had decreased; many technicians of the old school had come over to positions of sympathy with the régime. It was necessary therefore 'to show them greater attention and solicitude, to display more boldness in enlisting their co-operation'.[94] RAPP, which had shown a hostility to non-proletarian writers analogous to the 'specialist baiting' in industry, and in whose periodical even Gorky had been described as 'the bulwark and cover of the whole reactionary part of Soviet literature',[95] was dissolved by party decree on April 23, 1932.

On the basis of this decree a single 'Union of Soviet Writers with a Communist fraction therein' was set up in place of RAPP and all other literary groups.[96] Socialist realism was proclaimed in 1932 as the proper style for Soviet literature. It was defined in the Statute of the Union of Soviet Writers in 1934 as:

'The creation of works of high artistic significance, saturated with the heroic struggles of the world proletariat and with the grandeur of the victory of Socialism, and reflecting the great wisdom and heroism of the Communist Party, ... the creation of works of art worthy of the great age of Socialism.'[97]

Both organisationally and ideologically, Soviet literature was henceforward harnessed to the party and the State.

HISTORY

'The guiding principle' of Soviet historiography, according to the *Large Soviet Encyclopedia*, 'is the principle of Communist partisanship'. In practice, this means that usefulness to the party, rather than the pursuit of truth, must be the first duty of the Soviet historian. The years since about 1929 have been marked by a number of steps taken to ensure that Soviet historians should not neglect this task.

For some years after the Revolution, however, there were, effectively, two schools of Soviet historiography. Traditional scholarship found a centre in the Institute of History, founded under the *aegis* of Moscow University in 1921. And even when, in 1925, this institute was transferred to a new body organised under Communist auspices—the Russian Association of Scientific Institutes for Research in the Social Sciences, or RANION from its Russian initials—its work was still largely directed by non-Marxist historians. At the same time the few Marxist historians active before the Revolution, notably M. N. Pokrovsky, were precipitated into eminence. Pokrovsky became Deputy People's Commissar for Education, and was put in charge of the Communist Academy (the source of official doctrine in many fields), the Society of Marxist Historians (founded in 1925), the history section of the Institute of Red Professors (founded in 1921), and of the Central Archives.[98]

The Marxists and the traditional historians co-existed on the basis of a division of labour according to subject matter. Pokrovsky's declared thesis was that 'history is politics projected into the past',[99] and the Marxist historians' attention at this period was largely concentrated on the antecedents of the Soviet régime. The specialised Marx-Engels and Lenin Institutes, founded in 1920 and 1923 respectively,[100] pursued the hagiography of their eponymous revolutionary heroes.

Meanwhile the RANION historians devoted most of their attention to the more distant past. At this stage the Marxists showed little interest in earlier periods, Pokrovsky himself being exceptional. The traditional historians suffered not so much from competition from Marxists in their own fields as from the fact that the Marxists took the lion's share of such materials and resources as the State was prepared to allocate. 'The political history of past ages', said a survey of Soviet historiography of 1928, '. . . has remained in the hands of non-Marxist historians and *has not found its full expression in print . . .*'.[101]

It was not long before more direct pressures were brought to bear. In 1928 it was still possible for a Marxist historian to include RANION and the Society for Russian History and Antiquities (a survival from pre-war days) in a list of organisations which could be expected to further Soviet historiography.[102]

And Soviet historians of both Marxist and non-Marxist persuasions attended international historical conferences in Berlin and Oslo that year.[103]

This, however, was the last year in which such a state of affairs could exist. Historians, no less than other intellectuals, were affected by the Communist Party's general offensive against anyone to whom the label 'class enemy' could be attached. Such distinguished figures as Tarlé and Platonov, among the traditional historians, were attacked at a congress of historians, as 'class enemies on the historical front',[104] and sent into exile. The RANION Institute of History was transferred to the Communist Academy and its periodical publication ceased to appear.[105] The fateful consequences to Party history and its historians of the letter written by Stalin in 1931 to the periodical *Proletarian Revolution* were to be pointed out many years later by Soviet historians themselves.[106]

Pokrovsky emerged as the unchallenged leader of the Soviet historical profession; but his triumph was brief. His death in 1932 was followed two years later by the official condemnation of his doctrines on history by Stalin and Molotov, on behalf of Party Central Committee and the *Sovnarkom*, as 'abstract sociological schemes'.[107] In 1936 the anathema was repeated with greater force. Pokrovsky's views were said to be the basis of 'anti-Marxist, anti-Leninist, . . . anti-scientific views on history, . . . harmful tendencies and attempts to liquidate history as a science.. . .'[108] In 1939 the Academy of Sciences published a 500-page volume entitled *Against M. N. Pokrovsky's Historical Conception*, under the editorship of a former pupil, A. L. Sidorov.[109]

Pokrovsky, in fact, had been saved by his timely death from going the way of many another Old Bolshevik, for what is useful in disrupting tradition becomes not only superflous but dangerous when a new order is established. According to a volume of the *Large Soviet Encyclopedia* published in 1955, Pokrovsky

'tried to create a Marxist conception of the Russian historical process. However, he did not succeed in going any further than economic materialism, and failed to master historical materialism . . . [He] was guilty of vulgarising Marxism. . . . He did not understand the objective regularities of historical development, the two sides of social production, the dialectics of the development of the productive forces and productive relationships, the connection of the class struggle with the economic development of the country, the active rôle of the superstructure in social development, the creative rôle of the masses and the rôle of the individual in history . . .'.[110]

These elaborate phrases camouflage a simple fact. Until the mid-1930s the Soviet régime tended to justify itself by reference to its revolutionary aspirations for the future, to the exclusion of any appeal to national tradition. Pokrovsky's approach to Russian history fully accorded with this policy. The builders of the Russian Empire, notably Peter ('whom fawning historians have called the Great') and Catherine ('this dissolute and criminal woman') were treated as despots and intriguers without merit or virtue.[111] As the Stalinist State grew, however, and the prospects of world revolution receded, and as, due to the rise of Hitler, national defence came to the forefront again, such historical iconoclasm had to be discarded.

Patriotism, long regarded as a heresy in the Soviet Union, was restored to favour. The decree on the teaching of history, in which Pokrovsky's ideas were condemned, was published on May 15, 1934, and on June 8 of that year the Central Executive Committee promulgated a 'Law on the Betrayal of the Motherland', which added high treason to counter-revolutionary activities as a crime.[112] The law contained in its title and text the word *rodina* (Motherland), with all the evocative and patriotic overtones inherent in it. On June 9 *Pravda* published a leading article on patriotism, restoring to honour the word 'patriot', summoning all Soviet citizens 'to the struggle for the Motherland, for its honour, fame, power and prosperity', and concluding that 'the defence of the Motherland is the supreme law of life'.

In saying that history is politics projected into the past, Pokrovsky had spoken more truly than he knew. But if the reversion to patriotism for political reasons in the mid-1930s led to the eclipse of Pokrovskian history, it allowed at least some of the historians, such as Academicians Gotye* and Tarlé, who had suffered under Pokrovsky, to regain their positions to some extent.

* The name is a russified form of Gauthier.

[39]

SOURCES

1. *B.S.E.*, 1st edn., Vol. 34, p. 188.
2. *Preobrazhensky*, pp. 116ff.
3. *Ibid.*, p. 251.
4. Leontyev and Khmelnitskaya, p. 91.
5. *Ibid.*, p. 97.
6. Kondratyev, quoted in Dobb, p. 329.
7. *Ibid.*, p. 327.
8. *Strumilin*, quoted in Brutskus, p. 124.
9. Dobb, p. 323.
10. *B.S.E.*, 1st edn. Vol. 34, p. 154.
11. *Loc. cit.*
12. *B.S.E.*, 1st edn., Vol. 19, pp. 436f.
13. *B.S.E.*, 2nd edn., Vol. 50, Index of Names, pp. 735f.
14. *B.S.E.*, 1st edn., Vol. 63, p. 290.
15. *Loc. cit.*
16. Zenkovsky, Vol. II, p. 761.
17. *B.S.E.*, 1st edn., Vol. 24, p. 524; Hecker, pp. 151f. A useful account of Deborin's place in the controversy and his subsequent eclipse is contained in *Revisionism: Essays on the History of Marxist Ideas*, ed. L. Labedz (Allen and Unwin, London, 1962), pp. 126f.
18. Engels, p. 35.
19. Hecker, pp. 158f.
20. *Pod Znamenem Marksizma*, No. 5, 1929, quoted in Bauer, p. 26.
21. *Vestnik Kommunisticheskoi Akademii*, 1929, No. 33/3, quoted in Bauer, p. 26.
22. Stalin, p. 389.
23. Hecker, p. 176.
24. *Ibid.*, pp. 177f.
25. *Pravda*, August 2, 1930.
26. *Loc. cit.*
27. Hecker, pp. 180ff.
28. *Loc. cit.*
29. *Ibid.*, p. 187.
30. *B.S.E.*, 1st edn., Vol. 38, p. 829.
31. *Loc. cit.*; Fogelevich, pp. 11–12.
32. Fogelevich, p. 12.
33. Hecker, p. 187.
34. *Nat Literaturnom Postu*, No. 22, 1931, quoted in Brown, p. 179.
35. *B.S.E.*, 1st edn., Vol. 47, p. 524; Bauer, p. 56.
36. *B.S.E.*, 1st edn., Vol. 47, p. 524.
37. Bauer, p. 52.
38. K. N. Kornilov (1924), quoted *ibid.*, p. 61.
39. Kornilov (1923), quoted *ibid.*, p. 69.
40. Kornilov (1928), quoted *ibid.*, p. 70.
41. *Ibid.*, pp. 75f.
42. *Ibid.*, p. 82.
43. *Ibid.*, p. 80n.
44. *Ibid.*, p. 83.
45. B. M. Teplov (1947), quoted *ibid.*, p. 75.
46. Luriya, quoted *ibid.*, p. 74.
47. A. B. Zalkind (1924), quoted *ibid.*, p. 73.
48. Rozental and Yudin, pp. 47, 374.
49. Zalkind (1929), quoted in Bauer, p. 63.
50. *Loc. cit.*
51. *Psikhologiya* IV (1931), No. 1, quoted in Bauer, p. 96.

52. *Ibid.*, quoted in Bauer, p. 97.
53. Zalkind (1930), quoted *ibid.*, p. 99.
54. *Loc. cit.*
55. M. Efimov (1931), quoted *ibid.*, p. 112.
56. *Boldyrev*, p. 193.
57. *Ibid.*, pp. 191f.
58. Stalin, p. 661.
59. S. L. Rubinshtein (1946), quoted in Bauer, p. 149.
60. *Ibid.*, p. 121.
61. *Ibid.*, p. 119. However, unpublished research was done: *see* Problems of Communism, November–December 1965, p. 50.
62. Lenin, Vol. 10, p. 27.
63. *Ibid.*, p. 30.
64. Voronsky (1924), summarised in Struve, pp. 75f.
65. Voronsky, quoted in Brown, p. 25.
66. Voronsky (1923), quoted *ibid.*, p. 26.
67. *Loc. cit.*
68. Voronsky (1923), quoted *ibid.*, p. 27.
69. *Na Postu*, quoted in Struve, p. 73 and Brown, p. 20.
70. *Na Postu* (1923), quoted in Brown, p. 30.
71. Lenin, Vol. 29, pp. 308, 343; Vol. 30, p. 353; Vol. 31, pp. 291f.
72. Brown, pp. 19, 28.
73. Fogelevich, pp. 47–48, point 4.
74. *Ibid.*, p. 48, point 5.
75. *Ibid.*, p. 48, point 6.
76. *Ibid.*, p. 49, point 11.
77. *Ibid.*, p. 48, point 9.
78. *Ibid.*, pp. 48–49, point 10.
79. *Ibid.*, p. 49, point 12.
80. *Ibid.*, pp. 49–50, point 14.
81. *Ibid.*, points 14, 15.
82. Lunacharsky (1928), quoted in Brown, pp. 54f.
83. *Pravda*, December 4, 1929, quoted in Brown, p. 262.
84. *O Partiinoi i Sovetskoi Pechati*, pp. 380f.
85. *Pravda*, February 17, 1930, quoted in Brown, pp. 90f.
86. *Pravda*, April 19, 1931, quoted *ibid.*, p. 91.
87. *O Partiinoi i Sovetskoi Pechati*, p. 419.
88. *Ibid.*, p. 422.
89. Brown, p. 91.
90. Brown, p. 95.
91. *Pravda*, May 18, 1931, quoted *ibid.*, p. 95.
92. Brown, p. 99.
93. *Pravda*, December 21, 1931, quoted *ibid.*, p. 191.
94. Stalin, p. 476.
95. Timofeev and Dementev, p. 60.
96. Fogelevich, p. 50.
97. Quoted in Struve, p. 239.
98. *B.S.E.*, 1st edn., Vol. 45, p. 859.
99. *Ibid.*, 2nd edn., Vol. 33, p. 492.
100. *Ibid.*, 2nd edn., Vol. 18, p. 225.
101. Italics added. From: *Obshchestvennye Nauki SSSR 1917–27* (Social Sciences of the USSR, 1917–27), 'Educational Worker' Publishing House, Moscow, 1928, p. 156 (article by M. V. Nechkina).
102. *Ibid.*, p. 160.
103. Black, p. 7.
104. Zaidel and Tsvibak, *passim*.
105. Black, p. 7.
106. *Vsesoyuznoe Soveshchanie Istorikov*, pp. 19, 75, 363.
107. Boldyrev, Vol. 1, p. 170.
108. *Ibid.*, p. 183.

109. *Vsesoyuznoe Soveshchanie Istorikov*, pp. 368f.
110. *B.S.E.*, 2nd Edn., Vol. 33, p. 492.
111. Pokrovsky, pp. 119, 122.
112. *Ugolovny Kodeks RSFSR*, 1953, pp. 26f (art. 58[1a]). The law has since been revised (article 64 of the current RSFSR Code).

III

The System of Restriction

'Assassination', said Bernard Shaw, 'is the extreme form of censorship.' The Soviet State and Communist Party have used many forms of censorship, including the extreme form of physical 'liquidation' (inside or outside the law) to prevent citizens from learning or expressing thoughts which they consider contrary to their interests. The religious persecutions and the purges of the 1930s are examples of censorship in its most violent form. All restrictions of freedom tend to restrict freedom of thought; many of those which operate in Soviet society are described elsewhere.

The most immediate form of curtailment of freedom of thought, however, lies in restrictions on freedom of expression and information. These restrictions are enforced in the Soviet Union by a number of State censorship agencies, of which one of the most important is the Chief Administration for the Preservation of State Secrets in the Press, commonly known by is abbreviated Russian title of *Glavlit*.

Glavlit was formed in 1922, its terms of reference were changed several times during the 1920s and then given definitive formulation in a decree issued by the RSFSR *Sovnarkom* in June 1931. Its functions today derive, so far as is known, from this decree, in which it was laid down that the duty of *Glavlit* was to

'exercise all aspects of politico-ideological, military and economic control [*i.e.* censorship] over productions of the Press, manuscripts, photographs, pictures, etc. intended for publication or distribution, and also over radio broadcasts, lectures and exhibitions'.[1]

To this end the organisation was ordered to

'prohibit the issue, publication and distribution of works which
  (*a*) contain agitation and propaganda against the Soviet régime and the dictatorship of the proletariat;

(*b*) disclose State secrets;
(*c*) arouse nationalistic and religious fanaticism;
(*d*) have a pornographic character.'[2]

Glavlit's functions were defined as follows:

'(*a*) general guidance and inspection of local organs and plenipotentiaries of *Glavlit*;
(*b*) preliminary and subsequent control [*i.e.* censorship] over published literature, both from the politico-ideological and from the military and economic points of view, and also over radio broadcasts, lectures and exhibitions;
(*c*) confiscation of publications not suitable for distribution;
(*d*) issuance of permits for the opening of publishing houses and periodicals, the closing of publishing houses and publications, the prohibition of and permission for the import from abroad and export abroad of literature, pictures, etc., in accordance with current regulations;
(*e*) publication of rules, directives and instructions on subjects within its competence, which are binding on all institutions, organisations, and individual persons;
(*f*) investigation of complaints against decisions of local organs and plenipotentiaries of *Glavlit*;
(*g*) compilation, together with the appropriate departments, of lists of information which, by reason of its content, is a specially guarded State secret and not to be published or promulgated;
(*h*) preparation of list of works that are prohibited for publication and distribution;
(*i*) calling to account persons contravening the requirements of *Glavlit* and its organs and plenipotentiaries.'[3]

The key figure in the *Glavlit* hierarchy is the 'plenipotentiary' —the official immediately responsible for censorship at lowest level. These personnel, according to the 1931 decree, exist in 'publishing houses, the editorial offices of periodicals, printing establishments, radio broadcasting organisations, telegraph agencies, Customs houses, head post offices, and similar institutions'.[4] ('Similar institutions' may be supposed to mean large libraries, scientific institutions, certain major universities, various specialised agencies such as *Mezhdunarodnaya Kniga*, which organises the importation of foreign publications, and possibly the Union of Soviet Societies of Friendship and Cultural Relations with Foreign Countries,* which deals with foreign cultural contacts.) The plenipotentiaries were appointed and transferred by *Glavlit*, but maintained at the expense of the organisations to which they were attached; it was they who exercised 'preliminary' censorship.[5] The 1931 decree did not state who was responsible for 'subsequent' censorship at local level, but at the centre it used to be the task of the central *Glavlit*, the *Agitprop* department,† the Ministry of Internal Affairs and the Ministry of Defence.[6]

The distinction between 'preliminary' and 'subsequent' censorship was still being made in 1955.‡

Boris Polevoy's statement to an American periodical in 1955 the '*Glavlit* does not have censorship functions' was designed for foreign consumption only.[7] In fact, *Glavlit's* continuing responsibility for determining which books shall be 'removed from circulation' in libraries was proved by a decree of the Party Central Committee of October, 1956.[8] In 1959, another decree made *Glavlit* and its local organs responsible for reporting to Party organisations breaches of the regulations concerning free handouts.[9] That *Glavlit* is still concerned with the examination of material crossing the frontier is demonstrated by the new (1964) Customs Code: Article 72 refers to 'articles liable to examination by *Glavlit* organs' which are to be released by Customs establishments 'in accordance with the rules confirmed by the Ministry of External Trade'.[10] The categories of 'articles liable to examination' have presumably derived from those listed in the 'Rules for the Passage over the Frontier of Articles subject to inspection by *Glavlit*', laid down by the Commissar of Trade in 1929. The first of the Rules read:

'All productions of the Press, photographic blocks, sets of type, matrices, sound recordings, gramophone records, cylinders, disks and sheets of music for automatic playing on musical instruments, metal counters and badges, coats-of-arms, banners with inscriptions, sculptured figures, bas-reliefs, photographs, films, photographic plates, negatives, light-sensitive paper, manuscripts, documents, plans, drawings, artistic pictures, and sheet music, both for import and export, are subject to inspection by representatives of *Glavlit*.'[11]

These representatives decided whether or not the articles could be imported or exported. Where permission was refused, the articles could either be returned to the foreign country from which they came, or they could be 'passed on for use'—official use, presumably—'within the USSR', provided that the *Glavlit* representatives did not demand that they be surrendered to

° The body which succeeded *VOKS* in 1958.
† *See* pp. 97f.   ‡ *See* p. 49.

them for disposal.[12] *Glavlit* findings about the works of Sinyavsky and Daniel, published abroad under the pseudonyms of
Tertz and Arzhak (see Appendix II, p. 157) were apparently
read out at their trial.[13]

An early instruction by *Glavlit* made it clear that Soviet publications could also figure on the censors' black list.[14] For instance,
historical works not yet re-written to the latest Party line might
well be blacklisted. It is possible that the Secret Police still
help the censors to maintain this list. In 1922, the GPU was
charged with combating the importation and distribution of
books forbidden by *Glavlit*, and if it came across any works
not on the black list which it thought should be included, it
was to bring them to the censors' notice.[15]

Thus one of the censors' main concerns is to prevent the
importation of any printed matter held to be subversive. Ironically, vigilance has been directed not only towards 'imperialist'
countries in recent years, but also towards 'fraternal' China. In
1963 there were indignant Soviet reports about the smuggling
of Chinese publications into the USSR *via* parcels or suitcases
with double bottoms.[16] Frontier incidents occurred during
which Chinese citizens possessing 'publications of a character
hostile to the USSR whose import into the Soviet Union is forbidden in accordance with the Customs laws and regulations
in force' were expelled.[17] A Yugoslav lecturer complained of
Soviet censorship in 1965, after two copies of an article (published in Yugoslavia) which he had sent to Soviet writers had
failed to arrive.[18]

Glavlit, which originally formed part of the Ministry of
Education in each Republic, is to some extent masked by the
activities of the State Committee for Publishing attached to
the USSR Council of Ministers.* To judge by references over
the years, *Glavlit's* original full title 'Chief Administration for
Literary and Publishing Affairs' probably changed many years
ago.[19] Mention has been made of a figure entitled the 'Plenipotentiary of the Council of Ministers of the USSR for the
Preservation of Military and State Secrets.'[20]

Glavlit's internal hierarchy is obscure. Originally, within the
Ministry of Education, *Glavlit* was headed by a director under
whom there was a 'collegium'. The personnel of this group
was subject to confirmation by the Minister of Education 'in

* *See* p. 56.

[46]

agreement with the interested authorities'.[21] Although the latter were not named in the decree of 1931, they were given in earlier decrees on *Glavlit*.[22] The Ministry of Defence is probably still among them, but whether the MVD is still represented after its reorganisation is open to question.

Autonomous Republics, as well as Union Republics, have their own *Glavlits*, and organs of *Glavlit* also exist in *krais*, *oblasts*, and industrial centres with a considerable amount of publishing activity.[23] In each case the *Glavlit* conducts its work 'according to the directives and tasks of [the central] *Glavlit*.'[24] In *raions* the local Executive Committee 'in agreement with the appropriate organ of *Glavlit* appoints a special official to act as the local organ of *Glavlit*. These local organs —known as *krailit*, *obllit*, *railit*, or *gorlit* from the areas they control—are constructed in a manner similar to *Glavlit* itself.[25] A detailed account of *Glavlit* procedure was given by a former Soviet journalist in the British Press.[26]

Certain limitations on the functions of *Glavlit* were laid down in the 1931 decree. In the first place, material published by the former Association of State Publishing Houses (OGIZ), which used to handle the bulk of book publishing, was not given preliminary censorship by ordinary *Glavlit* censors. Instead, the directors of the publishing houses were themselves appointed *Glavlit* plenipotentiaries. For day-to-day control, they appointed from their staffs political editors (*politredaktory*) whose appointment was confirmed by *Glavlit*. Nevertheless, *Glavlit* could carry out 'in cases of necessity' preliminary censorship through 'specially appointed plenipotentiaries'.[27]

Secondly, publications of the Central Committee and *krai*, *oblast*, and *raion* committees of the Communist Party, the newspaper *Izvestiya* and publications of the Academy of Sciences, as well as publications by the Comintern and the Communist Academy, were exempted from ideological and political censorship by *Glavlit*.* In connection with the Academy of Sciences, it is interesting that a complaint should have been made in 1962 about the number of 'editors' then as compared to 1924. An historian described how a volume of an Academy of Sciences' regular publication, *Historical Notes*,

---

* This ruling no longer appears to have force except in the case of certain Party handbooks which, though 'signed for the Press', lack the censor's serial number (*see below*).

had to be examined by an editorial board and then a 'learned council',[28] This was not all.

'One of the comrades [*i.e.* possibly the *Glavlit* representative] had to sign a chit [authorising the work to go forward] to the publishing house, but he says: "I want to know if the second edition of the *History of the CPSU* has been cited." If we are to continue to watch over historians like this, we shall not free ourselves from the consequences of the Stalin cult for a long time.'

Even in the case of the exempted institutions *Glavlit* was obliged 'by means of preliminary inspection, to ensure the complete safeguarding of State Secrets'.[29] Appreciation of the scope of the regulations on State Secrets† suggests that this would be a full-time job.

Heads of printing establishments were (and are quite probably still) bound to submit to the *Glavlit* organs, for 'subsequent' censorship, five copies of every kind of printed work, immediately after printing and before public release.[30] All printing works had to bear the 'licensing visa' of *Glavlit* or its local organs,[31] and had to carry on their back page the number of the local organ or plenipotentiary of *Glavlit* who licensed it.[32] Until the late 1930s, this imprint used to take the form of the words 'Plenipotentiary of *Glavlit*' followed directly by the serial number (*e.g.* Plenipotentiary of *Glavlit* B 24884' on Vol. 32 of the first edition of the *Large Soviet Encyclopedia*, published in 1936); latterly, however, the censorship imprint has been limited to the serial number alone. For example, a book issued by the Publishing House of Political Literature in 1965, entitled *The Tale of a Chekist*, by V. Mikhailov, bears the censor's visa serial number A 10351. An academic journal, the *Herald of Moscow University*, Series VII, No. 5 for 1965, bears the censor's number L-27911.

With very few exceptions, every book, pamphlet, newspaper, periodical, etc. printed in the Soviet Union bears this stamp of censorship. The exceptions, apart from the collection of party documents and similar works mentioned above, are publications in foreign languages (which sometimes have a Russian edition, *e.g. International Affairs*) and a few periodicals printed in Russian but designed for foreign as well as for home consumption, *e.g.* the *Journal of the Moscow Patriarchate* and the *Fraternal Herald* (the Baptists' journal). This is in

† *See* Appendix I, pp. 61f.

line with the tendency, in operation since the 1936 Constitution, to avoid making public direct reference to the existence of censorship organs in the Soviet Union. Occasionally, however, there are signs of discontent on the part of writers. An article in the *Literary Gazette* of November 13, 1965 complained that manuscripts and even books 'signed off for printing' may spend an 'undefined time' at the hands of 'checking or advisory organs'.

CONTROL OVER PLAYS AND FILMS

Of the other censorship agencies, *Glavrepertkom*, which began in 1923 as a subsection of *Glavlit*, dealt with censorship of theatre, music, variety, the 'representational arts', gramophone recording and artistic radio broadcasting.[33] It also drew up and published lists of permitted and banned productions.[34] *Glavrepertkom* underwent a series of metamorphoses and changes in subordination. According to the *Large Soviet Encyclopedia* (Vol. published in 1955):

'From 1953 the functions of the Repertory Committee have been distributed between the Chief Administration for Literary and Publishing Affairs [*Glavlit*] and the Chief Administration of Theatres and Musical Establishments of the USSR Ministry of Culture (preliminary and subsequent entertainment control).'[35]

The control of these Administrations may well have been relaxed somewhat in 1956 when theatres were allowed to elect their own artistic councils, thereby gaining a measure of self-sufficiency.[36] They were also allowed to commission plays directly from dramatists. How restricted this freedom was in practice was shown by a collection of legal documents published in 1961[37] which stated that, in cases where 'organs of the Ministry of Culture' caused a play to be withdrawn before it was performed, the theatre was responsible financially for claims by the author, still outstanding at the date of withdrawal.

In 1963—the first six months of which were marked by a pronounced cultural freeze-up—it was suggested at a joint meeting held by the Ministry of Culture and the Union of Writers[38] that these 'artistic councils' should be expanded to include writers and representatives of 'public and creative organisations'. The implication was that orthodoxy should be injected where necessary.*

More overt control was actually reintroduced during the same year when a new body, the 'Repertory Council of the Ministry of Culture of the USSR' and various 'collegia' to supervise the repertoires of Soviet theatres were established. Proposals to tighten up control had been made earlier in 1963 and implemented in August. The announcement of the Repertory Council's establishment[39] described it as a 'consultative organ, co-ordinating the work . . . on checking the repertoire of dramatic (*i.e.* "straight") theatres' in Moscow and Leningrad—where most of the controversial productions had been staged. (The pattern was similar, however, in other Republics.[40]) One of the central Repertory Council's functions, as stated in the original announcement, was

'to work out recommendations on plays evoking contradictory evaluations. . . . The council's tasks also include the examination and confirmation of lists of plays . . . and dramatisations recommended for production . . .

The Repertory Council's decisions, confirmed by the USSR Minister of Culture, are obligatory.'

A. Kuznetsov, First Deputy Minister of Culture of the USSR, was appointed Chairman and another important official, G. Osipov, head of the theatre section of the Ministry of Culture, deputy chairman. Not much publicity has been given to the council's deliberations, but at one early session three plays were heavily criticised. One, *The Convent*, by V. Dykhovichny and M. Slobodsky, was considered unworthy of production by any Soviet theatre, and by the Moscow Theatre of Satire, in particular.[41] It was suggested that the appropriate cultural department of the Moscow City Soviet's executive committee should have a better look at repertory plans 'in the light of wishes expressed at the council's session'.

Another Ministry of Culture watchdog body, the 'Artistic Council for Dramatic Theatres attached to the Ministry of Culture of the USSR', was seen to function during 1964. It

---

* The 'artistic council' (*khudsovet*) of a theatre is concerned with the choice and production of plays. However, an article in the *Literary Gazette* of February 8, 1966 complained that it was merely a consultative body for the benefit of its chairman—the powerful director of the theatre.

appeared to have been in existence previously, for the membership of its presidia and plenums was 'expanded' for the first time that year. Its forthcoming activities were listed as follows: the first meeting of its 'new membership' was to be held in April to sum up the year in the theatre following Khrushchev's homily on March 8, 1963. The second, it was suggested, should be held in September, 1964, to examine 'the problem of traditions and innovation in the stage art of Socialist Realism', while the third, to be held in December, was to be devoted to preparing theatres for the 50th anniversary of Soviet rule and the 100th anniversary of Lenin's birth. The work of young producers was to be discussed at the beginning of the next theatrical season.[42].

The April meeting was, in fact, postponed,[43] but when it was eventually held one of the speakers was G. Osipov, who had the new title of 'Chief Editor of the Repertory—Editorial Collegium of the Theatre Administration of the Ministry of Culture of the USSR'. This collegium might well be carrying out the kind of 'preliminary' censorship which was *Glavlit's* brief according to the 1955 statement in the *Large Soviet Encyclopedia*. It is noteworthy that in 1964 the Ministry of Culture's Theatre Administration was held 'fully responsible for serious shortcomings which took place last season in the repertoire of theatres'.[44]

But despite all these precautions, some producers and playwrights still manage to slip heterodox work past the censors, both voluntary and salaried. This is because the tradition of 'Aesopian language' or innuendo is as old in Russia as censorship itself, and writers, artists, and producers are now adept in taking advantage of political lulls. Sometimes even the explicit instructions of such bodies as the Ministry of Culture are ignored.[45]

Other forms of communication were and are also still subjected to control.[46] In 1919, Lenin signed a decree nationalising the film industry. Soviet publications continually repeat—on the strength of one of his asides—that Lenin considered the cinema 'the most important' of all the arts.[47] The imposition of full control was delayed by resistance on the part of film producers and later by NEP (the New Economic Policy) and it was not until about 1925 that the Government gained real control over the choice of films being shown on Soviet screens. Even then foreign films formed the vast majority of those shown. 'It was necessary to introduce censorship, a task which Lenin imposed on the People's Commissariat of Education.'[48] The Government set up a number of its own producing organisations, including a film counterpart of RAPP.

Until 1957 there was no organisation corresponding to the Union of Writers. For instance, the cinema periodical *Iskusstvo Kino* was published jointly by the Union of Writers and the Ministry of Culture. But in June, 1957, a Union of Cinematographic Workers of the USSR * was established and given editorial control of the periodical (later to be shared with the State Committee for Cinematography).

This last body was created in March, 1963. Its head, Aleksei Romanov, was also First Deputy Head of the Central Committee's Ideological Department, and he revealed that the State Committee was 'directly linked' to the Party's Ideological Department (as *Agitprop* was then called).[49] These State Committees also exist at Republican level but two letters to *Izvestia*, on May 15 and 21, 1965, pointed out their uselessness. The writer of the first said:

'All scenarios and production estimates are first confirmed by the studio's artistic council and directors and are then handed over for the Republican Committee for Cinematography to inspect. But ultimately these questions are resolved by the USSR State Committee for Cinematography and thus the Republican Committees . . . are essentially some kind of intermediate link just for forwarding paper.'

The other writer confirmed this by saying that in Armenia there were almost two administrators for every person actually engaged in making films. Naturally

'. . . each of the administrators considers it his duty to give his opinion on the content of a scenario and on the footage that has been shot and on the selection of actors.'

Although Party leaders since Stalin have not gone to the latter's lengths in directly interfering with the shooting of films,[50] Khrushchev's outburst against a then uncompleted film entitled *Zastava Ilicha*[51] ensured that it was not shown until after his downfall, when it appeared with slight changes and

* The Union acquired a different name, the USSR Union of Cinematographers, holding its First (Constituent) Congress in November, 1965.

[52]

under a new title: *I am Twenty Years Old*. A writer in *Literary Gazette* of November 18, 1965 complained that the revised version, unlike the original, was 'dull'.

Film studios also have 'artistic councils' and 'scenario-editing collegia' which, like their counterparts in theatres, presumably weed through scripts in the first instance. Writers and critics as well as the studio's Party organisation, are supposed to take part in their work.[52]

The *Large Soviet Encyclopedia*, in its article on the hiring of films[53] says that this is a monopoly belonging to the Ministry of Culture and the function of the Chief Administration for Film-making and Film-hiring (*Kinoprokat*, or latterly *Glavkinoprokat*[54]). The *Encyclopedia* notes that this body must take account of ideological and cultural considerations on the one hand and economic ones—'the interests of the State budget'—on the other. Economic considerations have often had the upper hand in recent years, to the regret of Party activists who bewail the success of Western films and other cultural 'imports'.[55] Statistics show that the average number of people who see each new Soviet film drops 'unfailingly' year by year, according to an article in *Sovetskaya Kultura* on November 2, 1965.

Stalin left the Soviet film industry in very poor shape. In 1951, only nine films were produced[56]—but production as well as cinema building has been stepped up considerably in recent years. In April, 1963, *Tass* reported that more than 500 big cinemas were built in large towns annually. In the same year, 133 full-length films (including television films) were produced and 781 'shorts' (not including newsreels).[57] According to the Seven-Year Plan, 204 full-length films were to be produced in 1965, although only about 120 were made.[58]

Soviet film production itself has come under the control of various State bodies. A 1962 Central Committee decision mentioned the establishment of a Chief Administration for the Production of Films within the Ministry of Culture. 'All questions of cinema production, cinema technology, the financing of cinema studios and the training of cadres for the art of the cinema' were to be within its competence.[59]

Such censorship must inevitably stultify the 'freedom of speech' and 'freedom of the Press' promised in Article 125 of the 1936 Constitution, even though they are granted with the usual proviso—'in conformity with the interests of the working people and to strengthen the Socialist system'. Freedom of the Press, according to the Constitution, is 'ensured by placing at the disposal of the working people and their organisations, printing presses, stocks of paper . . . and other material requisites. . . .' In practice this means that only the 'organisations' exercise these rights and not the working people as individuals or as private organisations (in fact any group, however innocent, which dares to exist outside official auspices is still stamped on).[60]

Since the Communist Party ultimately controls all organisations, 'freedom' of the Press is non-existent in the Soviet Union. Even religious organisations, which might seem to offer an exception to the above statements since some of them publish their own journals, pay for their ideological independence by following the Party line in political matters. All newspapers and periodicals are the organs of some official organisation, and in many cases of some party body. Most regional newspapers are also mouthpieces of the local party organisations. *Pravda* for instance is the organ of the Central Committee of the CPSU, but the *Pravda* publishing house also prints five other newspapers as well as 27 magazines (some in various languages) and regular supplements.[61]

The party has all newspapers and sources of news under close control. The 'central information organ' in the Soviet Union is *Tass*. Details of its structure and working are given elsewhere, as are those of the *Novosti Press* agency, established in 1961.*

The limitation of the use of printing facilities to 'organisations' is enforced by a system of licensing by the Militia (police). In the 1930s, decrees were passed to ensure that[62] 'polygraphic enterprises and establishments' (which included all undertakings which either printed or bound or made print or printing machines etc.) could be opened only by State, co-

* See pp. 75f.

operative or public (*e.g.* trade union) organisations and only on receipt of a licence from the local Militia.

To acquire printing machinery they had to first obtain a further licence from the Militia, which was valid for three months. Even ordinary hand duplicators 'and accessories' could only be used by organisations having such a licence. This was issued in the name of the head of the organisation's 'Secret Department' or 'Secret Section', or, in smaller organisations, in the name of the director or of a person specially designated. The licence had to be registered with the local organ of *Glavlit*. These provisions still applied in 1946[63] but are likely to have been modified since.

CENSORSHIP OF THE POST

Apart from these restrictions, there are a number of measures controlling or limiting the Soviet citizen's access to information. Such freedom is not even guaranteed by the 1936 Constitution. The only remotely relevant provision is contained in Article 128, which declares that 'privacy of correspondence is protected by law'. But legal commentaries make it clear[64] that the examination and extraction of postal and telegraphic correspondence may be sanctioned by a *prokuror* [prosecutor]. In urgent cases, when the examination takes place without his sanction, he must be informed within 24 hours.

A recent novel by N. Virta, entitled *Swiftly Fleeting Days* contained a relevant aside about a letter which was 'deliberately not sent by post'.[65] Instead it was taken by hand from an important political figure in Moscow to the Deputy Prime Minister of a fictitious Republic who was engaged in political scheming. The implication to be drawn was that the appropriate authorities were keeping an eye on such correspondence.

Despite assertions of legality, a strong suspicion remains that sample letters are examined by censors. Mail to and from abroad is a particularly likely field.

PUBLICATIONS, SOVIET AND FOREIGN

The 'basic principle of the organisation of Soviet book-publishing and bookselling', stated to be 'radically different from the capitalist principle', is as follows:

'The principle consists of an *ideological trend* in the publication and distribution of books and the subordination of this matter to the policy of the Party and the interests of the working people.'[66]

Bookselling is controlled through the centralised book distribution system called *Soyuzkniga* (All-Union Book Distribution House) and subsidiary local *Knigotorg* organisations.[67] *Soyuzkniga*, in turn, is controlled by the powerful State Committee for Publishing (NB the Russian word *pechat* conveys both 'Press' and 'publishing' in general, hence references to the 'State Committee for the Press'—the same body). This was established in August 1963—under the Chairmanship of Pavel Romanov, previously head of *Glavlit* for some years—after considerable criticism of the book distribution system and of publishing.* The State Committee is responsible for the 'planning by subject, on a State scale, of the output of all forms of literature' and the compilation of detailed plans.[68]

Kniga-Pochtoi, another agency with branches in main towns, deals with mail orders for books. All subscriptions to Soviet and foreign newspapers, periodicals, etc. are channelled through *Soyuzpechat*, a Chief Administration of the USSR Ministry of Communications. The 1964 catalogue of foreign periodicals available to the Soviet citizen by courtesy of this organisation shows how restricted this choice is.[69] The only two non-technical publications listed from non-Communist countries were *Angliya* and *Amerika* (distributed in the USSR by Britain and the US by agreement with the Soviet Government). The contents of these magazines are closely followed and are liable to attack in the Press, on the radio or at gatherings.[70] All other (technical) periodicals were available only in translation or in reproduced form. The original contents can therefore be vetted as deemed necessary by the censors.

Foreign books* (and gramophone records) may only be imported through the *Mezhdunarodnaya Kniga* (International Book) organisation or, since 1956 for works from the 'people's democracies', through *Knigoimport*.[71] *Mezhdunarodnaya Kniga* is best known outside the Soviet Union as the agency for Soviet publications of all kinds, as well as for records and stamps.

* Romanov was replaced by N. A. Mikhailov, an eminent Party figure under Stalin, in 1965 (*see Vechernyaya Moskva,* November 2, 1965).

Strict control is also maintained on libraries and archives. Soviet historians have complained about the difficulty of access to the archives they need, although the position has improved of late.[72] The Director of the Institute of Marxism-Leninism, Academician P. Pospelov, has stressed that just because someone is doing research does not mean that he has the right to see unpublished Party documents in the archives.

'The Party archives are the property of our Party and only the Central Committee can dispose of them.'[73]

Another leading Party ideologue, B. Ponomarev, claimed that archive reserves are widely accessible, yet in the next breath spoke of 'closed reserves' (in the context of how access to them should be considered). He continued:

'If one research worker or another has a basis for assuming that interesting material, necessary for his subject, is contained in such-and-such reserves . . . the appropriate authorities should take a positive attitude in this matter.'[74]

From one of the resolutions passed at the end of the 1962 Historians' Conference, it was clear that catalogues and inventories even of open-access archives were lacking.[75]

The ordinary reader's access to works in the general part of a library is limited. Normally he must know the name of the book he wants before applying to see it. Neither the catalogues nor the shelves are open to inspection. The reader carries a card with full personal particulars. The library authorities have a complete check on all reading, as the order slip on which books are requested carries the reader's card number as well as his name and the titles of books required.[76]

Should a reader wish to look at any work which is suspect from the régime's point of view, there are further hazards. The main Moscow libraries (and probably all major Soviet libraries) keep controversial literature in a 'special store' (*spetzkhran*). It is difficult to gain permission to consult a work kept there and the supervision is very strict. There is of course no guarantee that the work required will even be there. For in-

* *See* p. 83 for the publication of foreign books.

[57]

stance, issues tend to be missing from stocks of foreign periodicals. References to these 'special stores' are rare in openly published Soviet sources, but A. Kravchenko, who edited an educational magazine in 1939 when Lenin's widow died, told how a part of her works was consigned 'to the special store sections of libraries' and another part 'consigned to oblivion and not republished' on the very day after her death.[77] Stalin had waged a notorious vendetta against Krupskaya, but the principle still stands. In due course Stalin's own works became 'the chief victims of the book purges',[78] and within days of Khrushchev's fall from power in October, 1964, his collected speeches were withdrawn from the bookshops.

There has been a large growth in the number of museums since the revolution.[79] Most of the existing ones are local museums and 'memorial museums' (where approved political and cultural figures are venerated). In 1964 the Central Committee passed a resolution 'On Raising the Rôle of Museums in the Communist Education of Workers'.[80] All museums, apart from the memorial ones, were henceforward to have sections

'on the Soviet period. . . . In the museums' exhibits, the successes of Communist construction in the USSR, the triumph of the Leninist course of the Communist Party, the struggle of the Soviet people to implement the CPSU programme, and the party's measures for the further development of industry, agriculture and culture, for the raising of the people's well-being should find their reflection.'

But even the Soviet Press itself has pointed out some of the absurdities of current museum practice such as the collection of personal relics from local notabilities.[81] An art expert has also revealed how difficult it is to examine museum reserves without 'a petition from an institution noting the theme of [one's] work', or without personal acquaintance with the museum director which allows 'private deviations from such a strict framework'.[82] He complained that the practice of having to present such a petition had spread from State archives to museums, and made it impossible for serious research workers 'to carry out wide-scale searches' as well as for the informed layman to satisfy his interests.

RADIO

Control over this most important communications medium has eased somewhat. Individual receivers at last are gaining ground as compared to loudspeakers wired to a local rediffusion station.[83] although as recently as 1957 there were 23,000,000 wired loud-speakers and only some 10,000,000 individual radios.[84] A close watch is still kept on amateur radio 'hams', however. (It was symptomatic that wireless receivers and transmitting apparatus had to be compulsorily surrendered within three days of the German invasion in 1941.[85] In March, 1945, a special decree authorised the return of, or compensation for, impounded receivers, but not transmitters.[86]) Short-wave operators need a licence from the Ministry of Communications, and these are not easy to acquire. Examinations have to be taken in various subjects and the candidate must build a short-wave set in order to get a first-class licence.[87] Radio 'hooligans' or 'parasites' who infringe regulations find themselves in court. Many of them are young people who transmit jazz, but there have also been complaints against religious communities for making 'propaganda' or just passing on the season's greetings to co-believers.[88] An indication of the seriousness with which the authorities view such behaviour was provided by a USSR Supreme Court decision on July 3, 1963.[89] This laid down that persons guilty of transmitting 'mischievous' broadcasts, or those which express manifest disrespect for society, grossly infringe public order or create obstacles to scheduled radio communications, should henceforth be punishable under Part 1 or 2 of Article 206 of the RSFSR Criminal Code (and the appropriate articles of Republican Codes) dealing with hooliganism. This lays down sentences of up to a year's imprisonment or 'corrective labour' or other penalties for a first offender and sentences of up to five years for repeated offences. The decision spoke of 'the heightened social danger of these crimes' and urged courts to consider the question of confiscating the apparatus used.

Another restriction, applicable generally to Western broadcasts until 1963, consists of jamming. This began in the Soviet Union, in 1949, and although for a few months in 1956 the jamming of BBC broadcasts ceased, it was resumed five days after the outbreak of the Hungarian revolt. It is significant that 1956 should have been the date of an argument about jamming in A. Chakovsky's novel, *Light of a Distant Star*.[90] A young man asks some highly pertinent questions about the need for jamming, *e.g.*

'Surely we can distinguish truth from lies ourselves?'

and

'If Lenin were alive, would he order these broadcasts to be jammed?'

For a short time in 1960 jamming stopped again, but was re-started on a new, selective basis when the Paris summit talks collapsed in May of that year. Thirty to 80 per cent of British and American output was jammed until 1963, when even this selective jamming ceased. (*Radio Free Europe*, broadcasting from Munich, continued to be jammed, and an American listener who had asked the reasons for this was answered by *Moscow Radio* with various irrelevances in August, 1964.)

This reduction of jamming was not to the liking of party-minded Soviet journalists and officials. The editor of a Lithuanian newspaper discussed the implications of the situation in these terms:[91]

'It is necessary to react in good time to various . . . occurrences, perhaps the unpleasant ones as well, which take place in our life. Otherwise what happens is that we keep silent and people find out about them from foreign radio broadcasts, in which case what they find out has an incorrect, distorted interpretation put on it. We still consider ourselves monopolists in the sphere of news. But this is not so. For sometimes, when we lag behind with the news, we involuntarily direct people to alien broadcasts, and if just any version is allowed to go the rounds it is difficult to terminate it later.'

Together with some relaxation in attitudes towards the West came acrimonious exchanges with China. Both the USSR and China extended their broadcasting services in order to concentrate propaganda on each other's peoples, as well as the developing countries of Asia. The Chinese accused the Russians of jamming their broadcasts in 1963[92] and the Russians counter-acted. V. Kulikov, an All-Union Radio 'observer' declared:[93]

'Chinese propagandists are carrying out truly piratical actions on the air, infringing the agreements between Socialist countries about the distribution of broadcasting frequencies; they crudely infringe other international agreements connected with the use of broadcasting equipment.'

[60]

Proof of Soviet interference with Chinese broadcasts came on July 30, 1964, when a programme running in parallel with *Moscow Radio's* second programme (*Mayak*) was transmitted for the first time on the same frequency as, and simultaneously with, *Peking Radio's* Russian language broadcasts. (Albanian broadcasts to the Soviet Union had been treated in the same way as early as 1962.) The interference—not identical with jamming but with a similar end result—was still going on some months later. *The Times* of November 4, 1964, noted a two-day break in this interference—a suspension of hostilities doubtless dictated by Chinese attendance at the October Revolution ceremonies. The blocking of Chinese printed and broadcast propaganda is a consistent, if ironic, development in the history of the Soviet régime's attempts to safeguard its subjects' ideological purity.

APPENDIX I

The following is the text of the latest decree on State Secrets in the Soviet Union:

'On the Drawing-up of a List of Items of Information which Constitute State Secrets, the Divulgence of Which is Punishable by Law.

Decree of the Council of Ministers of the USSR of April 28, 1956.

The USSR Council of Ministers resolves:
To draw up the following list of items of information which constitute State Secrets.

Information of a Military Character

1. Mobilisation plans and other documents containing summarised data on preparations for the mobilisation of the country as a whole, of the armed forces, arms of the service, military districts, armies, fleets and flotillas, and also of All-Union and Union-Republican Ministries of the USSR and enterprises of Union importance.

2. Summarised data on storage sites available and plans for stock-piling of all types of State and mobilisation reserves, and also of individual types of production which have a defensive or strategic significance in respect of the USSR as a whole, and of the Chief Administration of State Material Reserves attached to the USSR Council of Ministers and its territorial administration.

3. Operational plans, data on the location and numerical strength of troops, the amount of armaments and military equipment in respect of the armed forces as a whole, arms of the services, military districts, armies, fleets and flotillas.

4. General data on the combat-training of troops, and the state of discipline in respect of the USSR Ministry of Defence, the USSR Ministry of Internal Affairs, the arms of the service, military districts and fleets.

5. Summarised data on the numbers of servicemen subject to call-up on the reserve throughout the USSR, and the military districts, and also data on the bringing up to strength of troops by regular call-up, in respect of the USSR armed forces, military districts and fleets.

6. Plans with descriptions, diagrams and photographs of fortified areas, naval bases, central and district bases, and arms and ammunition depots, and also data on armaments and their equipment.

7. Summarised data on the airfield network, the condition and capacity of airfields throughout the USSR as a whole. Summarised data on defensive, airfield, base and special construction for the armed forces as a whole, and the military districts and fleets.

8. Plans of preparations for the local anti-aircraft defence of cities, major industrial, defensive and special objectives.

9. Data on the state of guarding the State frontiers.

Information of an Economic Character

10. Summarised data on the location of war industry, production capacities, plans for the production of armaments, military equipment and ammunition, and data on the fulfilment of such plans, expressed in terms of individual items, in respect of the USSR, the All-Union and Union-Republican ministries, chief administrations and enterprises of Union importance.

11. Summarised data on production capacities, plans for production of non-ferrous, precious and rare metals, and reports on the fulfilment of these plans, expressed in terms of individual items, in respect of the USSR as a whole, the USSR Ministry of Non-Ferrous Metallurgy, the Ministry of Non-Ferrous Metallurgy of the Kazakh Republic and their chief administrations.

12. Information on the USSR's underground resources of radioactive elements and their extraction; production capacities, plans for the production of radioactive and transuranium elements, and data on the fulfilment of these plans in absolute figures in respect of the USSR as a whole, and of ministries, chief administrations and enterprises.

13. Information on the size of unexploited reserves of non-ferrous, rare and precious metals, titanium, diamonds, and piezooptic minerals, in respect of the USSR as a whole, and of individual ministries, and information on major deposits; also information on the size of unexploited reserves of oil under the control of the USSR Ministry of the Oil Industry.

14. Discoveries and inventions of major military importance. Discoveries and inventions of major scientific and economic importance, before permission for their publication has been granted by heads of ministries and departments.

15. The state of currency reserves, information about the balance of payments, summarised data on State reserves and places for the safe-keeping of precious metals and precious stones, in respect of the USSR as a whole.

16. State ciphers.

17. Other data which may be included by the USSR Council of Ministers among information constituting State secrets.

In connection with the publication of the present decree, the Decree of the USSR Council of Ministers, dated June 8, 1947, No. 2009, 'On the Drawing-up of a List of Items of Information which Constitute State Secrets, the Divulgence of Which is Punishable by Law' is to be considered as being no longer valid.

SOURCE

Criminal Codex of the RSFSR published by *Gosyurizdat* (State Publishing House for Juridical Literature), Moscow, 1957, pp. 143f, passed for printing May 20, 1957, pp. 143–145.

SOURCES

1. RSFSR Laws, 1931, 31: 273, art. 1. (Reprinted in Fogelevich, pp. 124f.)
2. *Ibid.*, art. 2.
3. *Ibid.*, art. 3.
4. *Ibid.*, art. 4.
5. *Loc. cit.*
6. USSR Laws, 1939, 57: 689.
7. *US News and World Report*, November 11, 1955, p. 80. For a perhaps overstated description of *Glavlit's* declining powers, *see* Buzek, pp. 140f.
8. *Spravochnik Partiinogo Rabotnika*, 1957, p. 364. The reference is to a decree ordering *Glavlit*, together with the Institute of Marxism-Leninism, to look into

the question of restoring certain black-listed books on Lenin to the "open reserves" of libraries.

9. *Ibid.*, 1959, p. 542.
10. *Vedomosti Verkhovnogo Soveta SSSR*, No. 20, May 13, 1964, p. 380, art. 72.
11. Fogelevich, pp. 251–252.
12. *Loc. cit.*
13. London *Sunday Times*, April 17, 1966, pp. 21–30, pp. 33–34.
14. Fogelevich, 1927 edn., p. 34. For a detailed description of the kind of material black-listed in the 'thirties and of the workings of *Glavlit* generally at that time, *see* Fainsod, *Smolensk under Soviet Rule*, pp. 364f.
15. Fogelevich, 1927 edn., p. 32.
16. *Sovetskaya Belorussiya*, September 28, 1963; *Nedelya*, August 4–10, 1963.
17. *Pravda*, September 10, 1963; *The Times*, September 14 and 17, 1963.
18. Mihajlo Mihajlov in *Delo*, February 1965, p. 271 (trans. *The New Leader*, March 29, 1965, p. 38). This issue of *Delo* was itself removed from circulation by court order (possibly after Soviet pressure) and the author, a Yugoslav Communist of Russian extraction, prosecuted. See *Encounter*, June 1965, pp. 81f.
19. *Kharkov, Adresno-Spravochnaya Kniga*, p. 244; Fainsod, *Smolensk under Soviet Rule*, pp. 364–365.
20. Evtikhiev and Vlasov, p. 30; Fainsod, *loc. cit.* quotes an article written in 1934 by the USSR Council of People's Commissars' Deputy Plenipotentiary for the Preservation of Military Secrets.
21. RSFSR Laws, 1931, 31: 273, art. 6.
22. RSFSR Laws, 1922, 40: 461, and 1925, 71: 561.
23. *Baku, Kratkaya Adresno-Spravochnaya Kniga*, p. 81.
24. RSFSR Laws, 1931, 31: 273, art. 7.
25. *Ibid.*, arts. 7, 8, 9.
26. Sunday Telegraph, September 11, 1966.
27. RSFSR Laws, 1931, 31:273, art. 4.
28. *Vsesoyuznoe Soveshchanie Istorikov*, p. 333.
29. RSFSR Laws 1931, 31: 273, art. 5.
30. *Ibid.*, art. 11. That a similar process existed in 1958, and probably later, can be deduced from the Soviet source quoted in *Osteuropa-Recht*, September 1965, p. 177n. *See* also *ibid.*, p. 178n.
31. RSFSR Laws, 1931, 31: 273, art. 10.
32. *Ibid.*, 1931, 46: 347.
33. *Ibid.*, 1934, 10: 66 (Reprinted in Fogelevich, pp. 146f.).
34. *Teatralnaya Entsiklopediya*, Vol. 1, p. 1184.
35. *B.S.E.*, 2nd edn., Vol. 36, p. 396.
36. *Partiinaya Zhizn*, No. 1 1957, p. 37.
37. Quoted in *Osteuropa-Recht*, September 1965, p. 178.
38. *Sovetskaya Kultura*, December 24, 1963.
39. *Ibid.*, August 8, 1963, p. 2 and p. 1. For a general statement on repertory policy, *see Teatr* No. 10, for 1963, pp. 92–93. This stated that

'... the repertory plans of theatres, after being approved by artistic councils and the theatre directors, are confirmed by the Ministries of Culture or their organs, depending on the theatre's subordination'.

40. *Teatr*, No. 11, 1964, p. 97.
41. *Sovetskaya Kultura*, October 17, 1963.
42. *Ibid.*, March 28, 1964.
43. *Ibid.*, July 11, 1964.
44. *Loc. cit.*
45. *See* the 'highly instructive case' discussed in *Sovetskaya Kultura*, August 21, 1965.
46. *See Literature and Revolution in Soviet Russia*, pp. 199–200 for details of various decrees relating to plays, films, ballets, circus acts, etc. According to the terms of one of them, such productions were to be reviewed by the censors at least ten days before their official opening. In addition, two seats had to be reserved for the censors not further from the stage than the fourth row at every performance.
47. Quoted in *B.S.E.*, 1st edn., Vol. 32, p. 297.
48. *Ibid.*, pp. 307f.
49. *Pravda*, June 20, 1963.
50. *Ibid.*, October 28, 1962; *Censorship*, No. 2, Spring 1965, pp. 40–41.
51. *Pravda*, March 10, 1963.
52. *Partiinaya Zhizn*, No. 16, 1962, p. 38; *Kommunist*, No. 3, 1964, p. 64.
53. *B.S.E.*, 2nd edn., Vol. 21, pp. 36–37.
54. *Izvestiya*, January 31, 1964.
55. *Kommunist*, No. 3, 1965, p. 24; *Komsomolskaya Pravda*, September 3, 1964; *Pravda*, November 24, 1963. Statistics given by the Komsomol Secretary, Pavlov, in *Dvadsat Vtoroi S'ezd KPSS*, p. 148, show that where there is a choice, Western films are preferred to Soviet ones.
56. *Sovetskaya Kultura*, April 18, 1963.
57. *Narodnoe Khozyaistvo SSSR v 1963 godu*, published by the Central Statistical Administration, Moscow, 1965, p. 611.
58. *Stroitelstvo Kommunizma i Problemy Kultury*, Academy of Sciences' Publishing House, Moscow, 1963, p. 232; *Sovetskaya Rossiya*, November 23, 1965.
59. *Partiinaya Zhizn*, No. 16, 1962, p. 38.
60. *Sovetskaya Rossiya*, February 25, 1965; *The Guardian*, August 20, 1965; *Komsomolskaya Pravda*, June 7, 1962 and July 24, 1963.
61. *Preiskurant na Sovetskie Gazety*, p. 3.
62. RSFSR Laws, 1932, 64; 288; USSR Laws, 1935, 40: 341; Evtikhiev and Vlasov, p. 229 and note.
63. Evtikhiev and Vlasov, pp. 229f.
64. Studenikin, Vlasov and Evtikhiev, p. 278; *Nauchno-Prakticheskii Komentarii*, pp. 45, 287, 335. *See* also the article by P. Maggs in *Osteuropa-Recht*, September 1965, p. 175 for the sending of MSS abroad.
65. *Don*, No. 9, 1964, p. 13.

66. *Kniga*, p. 388. A detailed article on publishing policy in recent years may be found in *Soviet Literature in the Sixties*, pp. 150f.
67. Boon, p. 9.
68. *Politicheskoe Samoobrazovanie*, No. 2, 1965, p. 131; *Pravda*, September 15, 1964.
69. *Preiskurant na Zarubezhnye Gazety*, pp. 99f.
70. *Voprosy Filosofii*, No. 4, 1965, pp. 39f; *Molodoi Kommunist*, No. 5, 1964, p. 17; *Sovetskaya Belorussiya*, May 16, 1964.
71. Boon, p. 63; *Literature and Revolution in Soviet Russia*, p. 203n.
72. *Vsesoyuznoe Soveshchanie Istorikov*, p. 374.
73. *Ibid.*, p. 296.
74. *Ibid.*, p. 502.
75. *Ibid.*, p. 508.
76. Barghoorn, *The Soviet Cultural Offensive*, pp. 117f; *Soviet Studies*, January 1959, pp. 279f; *ibid.*, January 1965, p. 370.
77. *Vsesoyuznoe Soveshchanie Istorikov*, p. 260. On 'Library Purges' during the thirties, *see* Fainsod, *Smolensk under Soviet Rule*, pp. 374f.
78. *Literature and Revolution in Soviet Russia*, p. 202; *Osteuropa-Recht*, No. 3, 1965, pp. 178–179 on pulping out-of-favour authors.
79. *B.S.E.*, 2nd edn., Vol. 28, p. 494.
80. *Sovetskaya Rossiya*, May 22, 1964.
81. *Izvestiya*, May 21, 1964.
82. *Ibid.*, February 24, 1965.
83. *Pravda*, May 7, 1964; *B.S.E. Ezhegodnik*, 1965, p. 79.
84. *B.S.E.*, 2nd edn., Vol. 50, p. 415; *World Communications*, p. 367.
85. Evtikhiev and Vlasov, p. 343
86. *Loc. cit.*
87. *Moscow Radio* in English for North America, May 28, 1958. For the way in which 'hams' are organised, *see* *B.S.E.*, 2nd edn., Vol. 35, p. 531.
88. *Kazakhstanskaya Pravda*, February 27, 1965; *Komsomolskaya Pravda*, February 21, 1964; *Leninskaya Smena*, June 8, 1963.
89. *Byulleten Verkhovnogo Suda SSSR*, No. 4, 1963, p. 26.
90. *Oktyabr*, No. 11, 1962, pp. 64f.
91. *Sovetskaya Pechat*, No. 7, 1964, p. 10; *see* also p. 6; *Kommunist,* No. 3, 1965, pp. 16, 19; a few years earlier Surkov had spoken of 'a stratum of (mainly young) people who listen to broadcasts in foreign languages'. *Dvadsat Vtoroi S'ezd KPSS*, p. 306.
92. *New China News Agency*, March 3, 1963, quoting *Red Flag*. At a meeting of the International Radio and Television Organisation (OIRT) which opened in Bucharest on September 9, 1963, the Chinese even produced a tape-recording of alleged Soviet jamming.
93. *Sovetskaya Pechat*, No. 10, 1963, p. 58.

IV

State Organisation of the Press, Literature and Broadcasting

The system of restriction, by which the Soviet State controls its citizens' access to information, is paralleled by the system of inculcation, by which the State pumps into the citizens the information it wants them to believe. The entire machinery by which public opinion is formed is controlled by the State* and thus by the Communist Party which controls the State.

THE PRESS

The Soviet Press is described in the *Large Soviet Encyclopedia* as a Press 'of a new type ... the most revolutionary, advanced, and powerful in the world'.[1] The first Soviet decree on the Press, signed by Lenin immediately after he had seized power, apologised for the restrictions it contained—all hostile newspapers were, in effect, banned. This situation was stated to be

'of a temporary nature and will be revoked by special order once normal conditions have been restored to public life'.[2]

Neither Lenin nor his successors have shown any inclination to sign this 'special order'.

According to Lenin's dictum: 'A newspaper is not only a collective propagandist and a collective agitator, but a collective organiser as well.'[3] A periodical 'is a political utterance, a political enterprise'. Objectivity, so far from being desirable, is regarded as harmful: 'A periodical without tendentiousness is a ridiculous, absurd, scandalous, and harmful thing.'[4] Stress continues to be placed today on the need for a Press containing propagandist *publitsistika*[5]; the latter concept is defined in the

* With the purely technical exception of 'public' bodies such as *Novosti* (*see* below).

[67]

Large Soviet Encyclopedia as 'socio-political literature on contemporary topical themes. [It] always serves the interests of struggling classes and political groups.'

An enormous quantitative growth of the Press has been encouraged therefore by the Soviet Government. In 1927 there were 1,105 newspapers published in annual editions of 76,000,000 and 1,645 periodicals with a total issue of 229,400,000.[6] By 1965 there were 6,595 newspapers (in 65 languages) in annual editions of 98,000,000, and 3,883 periodicals of various types (*i.e.* including scholarly periodicals and bulletins) in combined editions of over 1,217,000,000.[7]

Newspapers and periodicals are abolished and created by the Party and Government. They may be abolished, amalgamated with or replaced by others, irrespective of whether or not they are finding readers. From January 1, 1963 a new weekly entitled *Literaturnaya Rossiya* (organ jointly of the Boards of the RSFSR Writers' Union and its Moscow Section) took over from the tri-weekly *Literatura i Zhizn*. Some central newspapers changed their titles and subordinations in 1960 and two military newspapers were abolished, leaving *Krasnaya Zvezda* as the daily Ministry of Defence organ. In 1962, following the March plenum, it was decided to abolish *raion* newspapers; this decision was reversed in 1965 and 'hundreds of new newspapers started to be issued'.[8]

A resolution of the 12th Party Congress (1923) included the statement that:

'It is necessary to create a particular type of newspaper for each basic stratum of reader.'[9]

This principle of specialisation is still a basic one.[10]

There are no independent newspapers. Every publication is described as the 'organ' of the Party, Government, or of other organisations and its subject matter is aligned accordingly. Textbooks on the Press still quote, by way of example, the 1939 decree censuring and dismissing the editor of a regional newspaper for publishing a polemical 'comment' aimed at the local *obkom*.[11] *Pravda*, the organ of the Central Committee of the CPSU, and *Izvestiya*, organ of the Presidium of the Supreme Soviet of the USSR, are both intended for the widest readership. Other central newspapers are for more specialised groups. For example, *Komsomolskaya Pravda* (organ of the Central Committee of the *Komsomol*) is for young people; *Trud* (organ of the All-Union Central Council of Trade Unions) is for trade unionists, which means, in effect, for industrial workers generally.

Such central newspapers dominate the Soviet newspaper world.* In January, 1966, *Pravda* issued 6,570,000 copies daily, a figure which includes the copies published from the matrices flown to a number of provincial cities.† *Izvestiya* issued 7,800,000 (the newspaper saw a considerable rise in its circulation under the editorship of Khrushchev's son-in-law, Aleksei Adzhubei). *Pionerskaya Pravda* published an edition of 8,210,000 and *Selskaya Zhizn* and *Komsomolskaya Pravda* over 6,000,000. Several other newspapers were above the 1,000,000 mark.[12]

Geographical specialisation begins below the central Press with the Republican newspapers, and continues below them with territorial and regional newspapers. Linguistic differentiation also appears at this point; for whereas the central newspapers are all printed in Russian only, the Republican and provincial Press usually appears both in Russian and the vernacular languages.

An example of a Republican newspaper is *Pravda Ukrainy*, organ of the Central Committee of the Ukrainian Communist Party and of the Supreme Soviet and Council of Ministers of the Ukrainian SSR. Unlike the central ones, party and Government are jointly responsible for publishing such Republican newspapers. One exception is the Russian Federation's newspaper, *Sovetskaya Rossiya*. When the Buro for the RSFSR was abolished at the XXIII Congress, the newspaper also dropped its subordination to Government bodies and became a CPSU Central Committee organ.

Corresponding vernacular newspapers are also published in the Republics, *e.g. Radyanska Ukraina* in the Ukraine. Other 'doublets' are *Sovetskaya Belorussiya* and *Zvyazda*, *Kazakhstanskaya Pravda* and *Sotsialistik Kazakstan*, *Sovetskaya Estoniya* and *Rahva Hääl*.

Where there are substantial minorities of a second, non-Russian nationality within a Republic, they may be served by a newspaper in their own language. In Tadzhikistan, for in-

* *See* p. 74 for 'circulation campaigns'.

† Most of the country receives the edition of *Pravda* prepared early the previous evening. However a later edition comes out the same night in Moscow and a few major cities (*Spravochnik Zhurnalista*, pp. 103–104).

stance, the Russian *Kommunist Tadzhikistana* is supplemented by the Tadzhik *Tochikistoni Soveti* and the Uzbek *Sovet Tozhikistoni*; and Georgia has daily papers in Russian, Georgian, Armenian, and Azerbaidzhani.

Although linguistic duality also persists to a low level in the local Press, during 1963 single editorial boards were formed 'in a series of autonomous Republics and *oblasts* where previously there had been one board for the local Russian-language newspaper and a separate one for the vernacular publication.[13] The editor of one of these 'unified' boards showed that the move was dictated to a large extent by ideological and Russian nationalist considerations.[14] Despite general protestations that this step marked an advance,[15] its usefulness was queried— especially where the editor of the twinned boards did not understand the language in which one of the newspapers was published.[16]

The functional groupings of the central Press are more or less clearly maintained at regional level. *Komsomol* and Pioneer papers, for instance, are issued in all Republics, *krais*, and *oblasts*.

Below the regional Press comes the local Press, falling into three distinct divisions—the *raion* and town papers, the 'lower' (*nizovaya*) or factory and farm Press, and the wall newspapers.

The *raion* Press forms a considerable part of the total number of newspapers printed in the Soviet Union. Normally these are the joint organs of the *raion* or town Party committee (*raikom* or *gorkom*) and the local Soviet. These papers are small in format and are published three times a week.[17]

They are frequently produced with poor printing equipment and are inadequately serviced by the news agencies.[18] Despite a 1959 decree aimed against losses incurred in publishing newspapers and magazines,[19] there is evidence that local papers which pay their way are exceptional.[20]

The 'lower' Press is the penultimate link in the chain. These papers are distributed at important construction sites, major industrial enterprises, higher educational establishments, and Government offices. Most are weeklies but in large enterprises they can be issued as often as three times a week. Of these *mnogotirazhki* (as these 'multi-copy' newspapers are often called), 2,627 were being published in 1964, the average circulation of each being 1,800. In addition, 1,528 *kolkhoz* newspapers were published with an average circulation of 700.[21]

Various decrees in recent years have tended to tighten up the regulations concerning *mnogotirazhki*, particularly as regards the numbers of full-time staff permitted.[22] One of the decrees ordained that the editorial collegia be stiffened with 'politically mature people'.[23]

Last of all come great numbers of typewritten, or even hand-written 'wall newspapers' (*stengazety*), produced and displayed in factories and shops, schools, farms, military units, and Government offices. A recent Party handbook stated that the local Party bureau must decide who is best suited to work on the editorial boards of these newspapers and 'recommends such comrades to the meeting' (which allegedly elects them). The book continues:

'The editor of a wall newspaper may also be a non-Party member if he is a mature, politically prepared comrade capable of pursuing the Party line.'[24]

The wall newspaper, states the handbook, 'has not got the right to criticise a Party bureau as a whole, opposing itself to the Party organisation'.

The wall newspapers are normally the joint organs of the primary Party and trade union organisations and may come out daily or as infrequently as once a month.[25] They are based entirely on local material, and are positively discouraged from extending their interest beyond their immediate bounds. The wider field is to be left to the printed papers,[26] and to the 'agitators' who harangue the people.* The wall newspapers' chief task is to urge workers to greater efforts by giving publicity to the successful ones and castigating the failures.

Other forms of wall newspaper are 'satirical or humorous' and have the same main purpose of encouraging greater productivity by congratulation or derision.[27] Thematic newspapers concentrate on a single subject and are found particularly in schools and other educational and technical institutions. Subsidiary forms of wall Press, such as bulletins, 'flashes' (*molnii*) and 'fighting sheets' (*boevye listki*) as well as a whole range of 'visual agitation'[28] are used as the occasion arises.

Soviet periodicals are also the 'organs' of specific bodies. The following table shows the annual circulation of some of the various types of periodical printed in 1964[29]:

* *See* pp. 113f.

Type	Total number of titles (including different editions)	Total annual circulation (thous. copies)
Political and socio-economic . . .	447	300,555
Natural Science and Mathematics . .	588	22,455
Technological: Industry, Transport, Communications, Municipal Affairs . .	1,100	235,025
Agriculture	327	34,534
Health, Medicine	305	30,914
Culture, Education, Science . . .	196	45,882
Literary and Artistic	196	338,054
Atheism, Science and Religion (*i.e.* Science *versus* Religion) . . .	7	2,979
For children	41	70,284
For young people	39	81,070
For women	36	124,216

The predominance of the Russian language is much more marked in periodicals. Of the 4,121 published in the languages of the USSR during 1963, no fewer than 3,240 (nearly 80 per cent) were in Russian.[30] There is also a lesser degree of localisation than in the newspapers. Relatively few periodicals—81 in 1962—are published in languages which are not those of peoples (like Ukrainians, Kazakhs, Latvians etc.) with Union-Republican political representation.[31]

Functionally, the periodical Press is as clearly divided as are newspapers. In many cases periodicals come from the same publishing houses as the newspapers. Twenty-seven come from the *Pravda* press[32] the most important being *Kommunist*, the Central Committee theoretical journal, and *Partiinaya Zhizn,* also sponsored by the Central Committee and aimed at a lower level of Party reader. (Most Union-Republican Central Committees also publish their own equivalent of *Kommunist,* usually in the vernacular, but sometimes also—or even only—in Russian). Young people's magazines, the satirical *Krokodil,* an illustrated weekly called *Ogonök,* the best-selling Soviet magazine *Rabotnitsa* (10,000,000 copies in early 1966) and even literary journals are among the others published by *Pravda.*

Ministries of the USSR and the RSFSR and other governmental and academic bodies are also important publishers of periodicals. Virtually all literary and artistic magazines are issued by 'creative unions', such as the USSR Union of Writers and its local branches. Propaganda magazines for abroad are produced in different languages by newspapers (*e.g. Pravda* publishes *Soviet Union* and *Soviet Woman, Trud* issues *New Times*) as well as 'public organisations' such as *Novosti* (see below) and the Union of Soviet Societies of Friendship and Cultural Relations (who publish *Culture and Life*).

In recent years, an attempt has also been made to channel the Soviet public's vast interest in life abroad into such safe channels as the periodicals *Abroad* and *Foreign Literature.* Particular care is devoted to the vetting of their contents.[33]

JOURNALISTS

Although the training of journalists is regarded as a matter of importance, it is heavily weighted with theoretical and historical studies.[34] Five universities—Moscow, Leningrad, Kiev, Lvov, and Sverdlovsk—have Faculties of Journalism.[35] Several other universities run courses in journalism, including correspondence and evening courses. However, professional standards continue to be low, as frequent complaints of plagiarism indicate.[36]

Yet it is a striking feature of the Soviet Press that it relies to a great extent on non-professional writers because it is required to be what is termed a 'mass' Press. As a result, a large part of the average Soviet newspaper is written by Party, governmental, and other employees, as well as by the 'man in the street' who has been increasingly encouraged once more to write letters revelatory of shortcomings and to proffer constructive proposals. A great deal of follow-up work is done behind the scenes on correspondence.[37] Nevertheless, only a tiny percentage of letters received are published. Occasionally, complaints come to light from people stating that letters have appeared above their names although they were not the authors.[38] The *rabselkor* ('worker and peasant correspondent') system of unpopular, trouble-shooting individuals, long characteristic of the Soviet Press, has declined somewhat in importance, now that carefully selected letters from individuals are allowed to make their points.[39] But *rabselkory* are still active and still unpopular: 349 cases of the 'persecution' of these snoopers were reported to a journal in 1964.[40]

When a newspaper has been written and printed in page proof, the editor reads the whole before 'signing off for printing'; this it would seem, is the moment when formal censorship

takes place. Editors are appointed as *Glavlit* 'plenipotentiaries' *
and 'signing off' is the last act in the chain of 'preliminary'
censorship.[42] The Party still keeps an eye on newspapers through
the 'Press Sector' of the Central Committee's *Agitprop*. In 1965
a case was reported in which the Sector's head travelled to a
small town on the White Sea following complaints about the
local newspaper.[43]

Distribution of the finished product is the function of *Soyuzpechat.*† This agency has a relatively small staff—45,000, about
half of whom man the kiosks etc.—but it relies to a great
extent on 1,200,000 Party, trade union, and Komsomol 'activists'
to increase the numbers of subscribers.[44] Campaigns to boost
circulation figures are a feature of the Soviet Press and under-
line its importance in the Party's eyes. Yet its overall dreariness
still surprises foreigners—even those from other 'Socialist'
countries.[45] Soviet journalists have themselves complained about
such aspects of their Press as its slowness in reporting events,
particularly when compared to Western practice.[46] A recent
editorial in *Kommunist* made the same point: 'Today, when
there is a radio receiver in almost every home, to remain silent
about a given event, not to elucidate it from the standpoint of
Socialist ideology, means giving "freedom of action" to the
falsifications of bourgeois propagandists.'[47] The article went on
to admit the 'high efficiency' of 'bourgeois information agencies'
and admitted that 'we are sometimes slow'. This slowness off the
mark is at least partially a result of the need to get items
approved for publication—*vizirovanie* is one of the terms
used.[48] Topicality is not helped by the need to place the 'correct' interpretation on the news. To take one telling example:
the outside world knew of Khrushchev's 'resignation' in October, 1964, before it was reported to the Soviet people. Other
matters of public interest are sometimes simply not reported. A
Soviet journalist has described the difficulties he encountered
in trying to report a plane crash in Leningrad.[49]

It is ironic that even 'exposures' of 'bourgeois' life—which
are all the Soviet reader is allowed, with very rare exceptions
—are themselves taken from Western publications and then
'processed', *i.e.* slanted, according to Adzhubei, *Izvestiya's* ex-
editor.[50]

* *See* p. 44.
† *See* pp. 56–57.

By far the most important of the State news agencies is *Tass*, the Telegraphic Agency of the Soviet Union. It is directly attached to the USSR Council of Ministers.

A decree of 1935[51] declared it to be the 'central organ of information in the USSR'. The decree granted *Tass* exclusive rights in the distribution of information about the USSR in foreign countries, in the distribution of foreign and All-Union information within the USSR and of all domestic information from one Union Republic to another. These monopolies were broken in 1961 when *Novosti* began to distribute feature material at home and abroad. Thus the only information which does not pass through *Tass* is *Novosti* feature-material and what news is deemed to be solely of Union-Republican interest. This is handled by the Telegraphic Agency of the Union Republic concerned. There are only 500 permanent *Tass* correspondents in the country as a whole, including those who work for the 14 Union-Republican news agencies outside the RSFSR (*e.g. Armentag* in Armenia, *Kirtag* in Kirgiziya).[52]

These agencies are similar to *Tass* in being attached to their respective Union-Republican Councils of Ministers, but the RSFSR is served by *Tass* itself, which has a 'plenipotentiary' attached to the RSFSR Council of Ministers. In fact, the 1935 decree ensured that the Union-Republican agencies should be nothing but local organs of *Tass* and completely subordinated to it. According to the decree, *Tass* 'exercises direction and control over the work of the telegraphic agencies of the Union Republics and gives them concrete orders for the collection and distribution of information; moreover [*Tass*] directives and assignments are binding [on them]'.[53] Furthermore, *Tass* 'trains cadres of staff workers for the entire system of telegraphic agencies'. The directors of the Union-Republican agencies are appointed by the appropriate Councils of Ministers 'in accordance with the representations' of the director of *Tass*.

Tass is headed by a director general who is appointed, as are his deputies, by the USSR Council of Ministers. The present head (since April, 1967) is S. G. Lapin, a member of the Central Committee who has held senior diplomatic appointments. He has been a Deputy Minister of Foreign Affairs and Ambassador in Vienna and Peking. Interchange between *Tass* and the Foreign Ministry is not unusual.[54]

Before 1954 Lapin had experience in journalism and broadcasting. For instance, he was Chief Editor for Political Broadcasts in the Council of Ministers' Committee for Broadcasting. *Tass* has three Deputy Directors and, since 1962, a twelve-man consultative collegium.[55]

Tass representatives abroad have frequently engaged in intelligence and other impermissible activities.[56] A Soviet writer has reminisced about a former MVD colleague whom he ran into before the war in Italy, where the latter was acting as a *Tass* correspondent under an assumed name.[57] In 1960, the *Tass* correspondent in Rangoon, Kovtunenko, was smuggled out to avoid standing trial and in January, 1963, the agency's representative in Oslo was refused a residence permit after being found trespassing in the offices of the Norwegian Parliament.

L. Solyakov of *Tass* was expelled from Kenya in March, 1966.* In January of the same year, I. Yakovlev, a *Tass* correspondent, had been one of five Russians expelled from West Germany for being implicated in scientific espionage (*The Times*, January 22 and 26, 1966). Although the number of espionage cases brought to light has tapered off in recent years, *Tass* remains a potential medium for intelligence activities. In any case, a great deal of the information *Tass* sends to Moscow is in the category of military, political, and economic intelligence.[58] The agency's personnel work in close contact with Soviet diplomats.

Tass has more than 100 foreign correspondents and its Moscow staff was almost 2,000 in early 1964.[59] At the end of 1965, there were correspondents and offices in 92 countries. The largest offices (in New York, London, Paris, Tokyo, and Helsinki) are connected to Moscow by a two-way teletype link which works round the clock. The agency has correspondents in all European countries except Spain, Portugal, and Luxemburg, in most Asian, Middle and Far Eastern countries and in 15 Latin American and 24 African countries. *Tass* has agreements on exchanging information with 37 foreign agencies and *Tass* broadcasts (in Russian, English, French, Spanish, and German) are translated abroad into Arabic, Tamil, Japanese, and other languages and given to recipients in printed form.[60] The head of the *Tass* chief editorial section for information destined for foreign countries has described how information is tailored to the traditions of the country concerned.[61] He stressed the need to put facts first and commentary last, thereby

* *See* p. 79.

[76]

indicating the rather different order of priorities outside the
Soviet Union. Apart from him, there are chief editors of foreign
news, Union (*i.e.* home) news, foreign broadcasts, Union broadcasts, and photo-news. There are also an editor of sporting
news, a group of commentators, an information section, and
communications departments. The agency also publishes a
variety of bulletins.[62]

One of *Tass*'s less publicised services is the provision of
news, a group of commentators, an information section, and
communications departments. The agency also publishes a
variety of bulletins.[62]

Soviet journalists have themselves criticised the agency, *Tass*,
notably Adzhubei, who emphasised:

'*Tass* information is extremely dry. . . . Sometimes foreigners write
about us far more vividly than we write about ourselves.'[64]

Other journalists have accused *Tass* of being cliché-ridden
and irrelevant to their needs, and of providing a poor service
for the radio and the local Press. The present head of *Tass*
admitted that there was some truth in the criticism that the
agency was slow compared to Western agencies, but put the
best face on this by saying: '*We do not put out rumours but put
out facts.*'[65] Sweeping claims are also usual, however, *e.g.* '*Tass*
information is the most truthful in the world'.[66] A standard
handbook (*Spravochnik Zhurnalista*, pp. 391–392) puts such
bombast into perspective when it points out that *Tass* and *APN*
material has to be checked 'without fail' as 'in many cases' it
contains factual errors. The Soviet view of truth and objectivity
was well defined by Palgunov, the agency's former head:

'Soviet information is distinguished by its accuracy and truth. It
is extremely objective. However for information to be objective does
not merely mean that it should confine itself to registering facts.
Soviet information not only adduces facts but analyses them in a
Marxist way as well; . . . it serves the cause of Communism, the
cause of fighting the bourgeois ideology hostile to us.'[67]

Even the speeches of State visitors are tailored when necessary. *Pravda* of May 2, 1964 quoted statements by the then
President of Algeria, Ben Bella, to the effect that religious be-
liefs did not stop Algerians from being friends of the Soviet
Union, nor from being revolutionaries. These phrases were left
out of *Tass* summaries of his speech published in Central Asian
newspapers a few days later. As there are large numbers of

Muslims in Soviet Central Asia, the deletions were hardly for-
tuitous. The *Tass* treatment of a speech made in September,
1956 by President Sukarno of Indonesia which referred to belief
in Islam had been exactly the same.

'NOVOSTI'

On February 21, 1961, a new Press agency called *Novosti* was
established. (It is also known as *APN*—the initials of *Agentstvo
Pechati Novosti* which literally means the 'News' Press Agency.)
Its sponsors were the USSR Union of Journalists, the USSR
Union of Writers, the Union of Soviet Societies of Friendship
and Cultural Relations with Foreign Countries, and the highly
propagandist All-Union Society for the Dissemination of Political and Scientific Knowledge.*

All these organisations—and hence *Novosti* itself—are termed
'public', but the Russians would be the first to admit to the leading rôle ideology plays within them. For instance, one of
the main tasks of the Union of Journalists is 'the raising of the
ideological and political level of its members'.[68] Article 9 of the
Novosti Statutes [69] claims that 'no Soviet State organ' bears any
responsibility for the agency's activities and finances. This claim
must be looked at in the light of the nominal sum charged for
Novosti services (which was roughly one dollar a month within
the Soviet Union)[70] and the highly professional way in which
the agency (equipped with expensive machinery) is run.[71] There
can be no doubt that its *raison d'être* is the provision of a world-
wide feature and publicity service which faithfully echoes the
official line—many anti-Chinese polemics have been published
under the *Novosti* imprint—yet is free from the stigma of the
'official' agency, *Tass*. The fact that *Novosti* works through the
Press Departments of many Soviet embassies abroad also helps
to belie its 'unofficial' pretensions. A recent UNESCO publication, presumably compiled from material supplied by the countries concerned, stated:

'[*Novosti*] bureaux are maintained in London, Paris, Montevideo,
Rio de Janeiro, New Delhi, Rangoon, Djakarta, and the socialist
countries of South-East Asia and Europe. Others are planned for
Tokyo, Tunis, Berlin, Cairo, and other capitals *where the agency
currently works through correspondents and uses the translation and
other Press faculties of the local Soviet Embassy.*' (Italics added.)[72]

* Restyled the *Znanie* or 'Knowledge' Society in 1963.

[78]

In fact, the New Delhi Bureau mentioned above closed down in 1964 and its functions were taken over by the Soviet Embassy's Information Department. *Novosti* from the first included important figures among its administrators, *e.g.* Aleksei Adzhubei (Chief Editor of *Izvestiya* until Khrushchev's, his father-in-law's downfall). It is not known whether Adzhubei is still one of the chairmen of the agency's Council of Sponsors; this is particularly unlikely as new ones have been elected.[73] Boris Burkov, who remains chairman of the *Novosti* Board, was described in 1960 as Deputy Chief Editor of *Pravda*.

In terms of expansion and quantity of output, *Novosti* has undeniably been a success, riding particularly high on the wave of foreign interest in Soviet space achievements and in Khrushchev, for whom the agency acted almost in a public relations capacity.[74] One example is characteristic of *Novosti's* growth. When it was established in 1961, it had two representatives in the whole of Africa. In mid-1964, it had eleven 'bureaux and correspondents' offices' and by the end of that year it had been decided to open another five.[75] At that time, *Novosti* had correspondents in fifty-six countries. The agency has some 1,500 writers working permanently for it,* and thousands of more casual contributors who have material published at least once a year.[76] A few years ago, it had nine Chief Editorial Boards which 'co-ordinated the editorial boards preparing material for Soviet publications abroad, for the Press of one country or another, for the Soviet Press'.[77]

There have been some setbacks, however. The fall of Khrushchev occurred just after the publication of a *Novosti* booklet in India containing many references to him. The booklet (entitled *President Radhakrishnan's Visit to USSR*) was withdrawn from circulation, and another entitled *Friendship Visit* substituted. References to the former First Party Secretary were scrupulously removed—even from the official text of a joint communiqué signed by India as well as the USSR, thereby causing offence in India.[78]

Yury Kuritsin of *Novosti* was one of a group of Communist diplomats and journalists expelled from Kenya for apparently 'using their positions as a cover for more political activities'.†

* An article in *Sovetskaya Pechat* No. 10, 1964 described *Novosti's* recruitment of specialist graduates.
† *The Times*, March 11, 1966.

In January, 1965, Boris Karpovich, a Deputy Chairman of the *Novosti* board, and an information counsellor at the Soviet Embassy in Washington, was expelled by the State Department for his implication in espionage activities a few years previously, while he was working at the United Nations Secretariat.[79] Later in the same year, it was reported that a Soviet journalist in the Oslo office of *Novosti* had left Norway to have his 'holiday' in the Soviet Union just before a spy trial. The office stated that he would 'probably not return'.[80]

On March 26, 1964, *Tunis Radio* announced that the Guinean Government had ordered *Novosti* not to distribute its bulletins to subscribers and the public as this might harm relations between Guinea and other African countries. A year later, in March, 1965, the Ceylon Ministry of Defence and External Affairs regretted that some diplomatic missions were contravening an earlier ruling and publishing bulletins which reproduced articles containing disparaging references to other countries. Although *Novosti* was not specifically mentioned, it frequently publishes bulletins of this type.[81]

It is interesting to note that Soviet journalists themselves have attacked those of their own newspapers which make too much use of *Novosti* feature material. (*See*, for example, the August, 1965, issue of *Sovetskaya Pechat*.)

In the main, however, *Novosti* has achieved an undoubted degree of success in providing newspapers and publishers in the West and in the 'uncommitted nations' with articles, books, and photographs on Soviet topics.[82] One result of the general reorganisation of Soviet publishing houses in 1964 was the establishment of the 'Publishing House of the *Novosti* Press Agency'[83] which puts out tendentious and even inaccurate booklets. A typical recent example was entitled *USSR: Questions and Answers* and contained such demonstrably untrue statements as, in answer to a question about unemployment: 'We have none'. *Novosti* is also concerned with other communications media. In July, 1964, the agency became one of the sponsors of *Radio Station Peace and Progress*, a new propaganda service beamed at Latin America.[84] *Novosti* also started supplying material for television not very long after its establishment and in 1964 a 'television news editorial board' was set up to fulfil foreign requests.[85]

Novosti also plays a part in such *ad hoc* activities as buying of space in foreign newspapers and sending them letters. During 1962, for instance, the full text of a speech by Khrushchev was placed in various British and Canadian newspapers. One of the latter, the *Winnipeg Free Press*, asked a Soviet newspaper which carries advertisements—*Vechernyaya Moskva*—if it would accept one in return. The request was refused. Similarly, letters are written by *Novosti* correspondents which present the Soviet point of view.[86]

Novosti 'public sections' in Republics such as the Ukraine produce articles especially designed for emigrés abroad (*e.g.* in Canada).[87] This forms part of the official Soviet drive to repatriate such emigrés.

All in all, it is not surprising that Soviet journalists themselves recognise the family relationship between *Novosti* and *Tass* and declare: '*APN* is the younger brother of *Tass*'.[88] As Burkov has stated:

'*Tass* and *APN* possess good possibilities for making propaganda for the successes of the Soviet people, for unmasking propaganda hostile to us.'[89]

LITERATURE

Literature, probably the most sensitive of all the indicators of freedom of thought, has suffered severely from the 'dictatorship of the proletariat'. Censorship under the Tsars was a model of inefficiency compared with the system of State and Party control erected by the Soviet régime. The beginnings have already been described,* the recent effects of 'Partyness' on literature will be dealt with later.

The single Union of Writers set up after the dissolution of *RAPP* and other literary groups in 1932, still survives. Headed first by Gorky, then by literary bureaucrats such as Fadeev and Surkov—the latter being succeeded by Fedin, a less authoritarian figure—the Union of Writers proved to be a relatively strong body of its kind, much stronger than, for example, the analogous Unions of Composers and Artists. Whereas from 1936 the latter were subject to the supervision of the Committee for Affairs of the Arts attached to the Council of People's Commissars of the USSR, the Union of Writers existed without any special government body to look after it. Even after the Ministry of Culture was set up in 1953, the

* *See* pp. 30f.

Union of Writers was not among those listed in the *Large Soviet Encyclopedia* as being under its supervision.[90]

The Party does, however, control the union from within (by the usual Party cells) and above. The latter function used to be carried out by the Central Committee's Department for Culture and Science, which contained a Literature Sector in touch with the union, editorial boards of magazines and newspapers and with publishing houses.[91] The obituary of D. Polikarpov, in *Pravda* of November 3, 1965, stated that he had headed the Department for Culture (presumably its present title) for ten years. More generally, the Union of Writers' ideological platform is restricted in that all members must adhere to the method of 'Socialist Realism'. This singular artistic-cum-ideological method has become even more difficult to comprehend of late because its proponents defensively insist that it comprises a variety of 'styles'.[92] Restrictions, therefore, tend to be negative. Official pundits know what they don't like and attack errant writers at public gatherings or in the Press.* Latterly, however, there have been polemics over what is permissible and what is not, sometimes at a high level.[93]

Since all Soviet literary journals and newspapers are the official organs of the Union of Writers or of its branches, it is axiomatic that members of the union have far greater possibilities of publishing their work in them than do non-members. And the same applies, *a fortiori*, to editorial posts on the periodicals.[94] Many other advantages accrue to members. The Literary Fund (*Litfond*) of the Union of Writers, whose revenues derive from various sources including the State Budget, is, as it were, the union's benevolent fund and ensures material assistance to needy members and their families, medical treatment (it maintains sanatoria and rest homes) and many ancillary services. Thus the benefits and perquisites which a Soviet writer stands to acquire are considerable[95] if he does not overstep the line. The importance of working within an accredited organisation could be seen from the trial of the young Leningrad poet and translator, Josef Brodsky, in 1964. The judge suspiciously inquired why Brodsky worked in isolation and did not belong to any literary societies.[96]

The State is, in effect, the only book publisher in the Soviet Union *via* the State Committee for Publishing.[97]

* See pp. 77f.

[82]

In 1952, the Ministry of Culture's supervisory department for all publishing houses, *Glavpoligrafizdat*, was divided into three chief administrations responsible for different sectors of publishing.[98] In 1959, a unified chief administration, *Glavizdat*, was formed with branches in the Union Republics down to *oblast* level.[99]

Every manuscript submitted to a publishing house has to go through a preliminary 'editing' even before the text reaches *Glavlit*. As the editors of publishing houses and periodicals are likely to be held responsible for the political deviations of any author they publish,[100] they frequently tend to be over-suspicious.[101] Although manuscripts no longer necessarily have to be 'reviewed' (discretion lies with those in charge of publishing houses), the first question a reviewer has to ask is:[102] 'Does the content of the manuscript correspond to the general line of the Communist Party and the Soviet Government, and are the ideological aims in it correct?' Khrushchev said it was no secret that certain individuals viewed the 'just advice and comments' made by publishing houses, periodicals, theatres, and cinema studios about the work they proffered for publication or production as 'rules and regulations which allegedly restrict them'.[103]

The publication of foreign works is also controlled with extreme care. In 1958, the Central Committee decided that its own *Agitprop* and Department of Culture would examine all plans for publishing foreign literature.[104] In June, 1959, criticism was levelled at the Foreign Languages Publishing House whose tasks were clearly defined in another decree. One section of the decree dealt with 'works by bourgeois authors' on 'philosophy, history, economics, diplomacy, and law'. There was a strong caveat:

'Such books must be published in limited editions; passages of no scholarly or practical interest are to be deleted from them; and they are to be supplied with lengthy introductions and annotations.' (*I.e.* to counter any heterodox thoughts which might still remain.)[105]

BROADCASTING

The radio, which Lenin described as a newspaper free from the restrictions imposed by time and paper,[106] has usually been linked with the Press both in Communist theory and practice.

[83]

Like the Press, Soviet domestic sound broadcasting is conducted at carefully defined levels.

'Central' sound broadcasting was first in the hands of a public joint-stock company known as *Radioperedacha* and later under the Commissariat of Posts and Telegraphs. From 1933 the controlling body was the All-Union Radio Committee or VRK,[107] until, in 1953, it was absorbed as a Chief Administration into the Ministry of Culture. In May, 1957, however, radio was detached from the Ministry and placed under a State Committee for Radio Broadcasting and Television attached to the Council of Ministers of the USSR. The motive underlying this reversion to previous practice was, in the words of the decree, 'the ever-growing importance of radio and television as powerful means of information, of mobilising the workers to solve the tasks of Communist construction, and of the political and aesthetic education of the Soviet people.'[108]

One of the four Deputy Chairmen of the State Committee is concerned solely with foreign broadcasts.[109] All recording equipment, incidentally, belongs to the State Committee (broadcasting and television studios etc. belong to the Ministry of Communication).[110]

The extent to which the Party regards itself as being the sole master of these communications media as well may be inferred, for instance, from the title of a recent CPSU Central Committee decree: 'On the Management of the Press, Radio, and Television by the Central Committee of the Turkmen CP'.[111]

A Deputy Chairman of the State Committee for Radio Broadcasting has his office in the All-Union Radio's 'Radiohouse' in Moscow where those responsible for the coming day's programmes meet daily. The previous day's broadcasts are also examined in great detail—especially if they contain any slips, however minor.[112] Among the Chief Editorial Boards represented on one typical day were those dealing with the 'latest news', political propaganda, natural science broadcasts, literary and theatre news, music, children and youth, local broadcasts, and broadcasts for Moscow and the Moscow *oblast*. The Chief Editorial Board for Programmes—a coordinating body whose members, among other tasks, 'read all the material prepared for transmission'—was represented by its Deputy Chief Editor.[113]

One of the more important of the Chief Editorial Boards, that of political propaganda—it was responsible for some 22

[84]

hours of broadcasts per week at the end of 1962—consists of a total staff of sixty-four.[114] One of its sections is responsible for the young people's programme called radio station *Yunost* (Youth)'. The fact that this section forms part of the Chief Editorial Board of Political Propaganda is not surprising in the light of the following injunction from an important Central Committee decree 'On the Improvement of Soviet Radio Broadcasting':

'The main task of radio broadcasting for children and young people must be the education of young patriots—ideologically armed fighters for Communism, implacable towards bourgeois ideology.'[115]

The writer, Sergei Mikhalkov, who became head of the Moscow Writers' Organisation in January, 1965, has told an instructive tale about a five-year-old child who said to his parents that it was not they who cared for him, but the party and Government. He had 'absorbed' this phraseology from the radio and television.[116] Mikhalkov went on to suggest that such 'Soviet consciousness' was best acquired at a pre-school age.[117]

Both the 1960 decree and another issued by the Central Committee two years later made it abundantly clear that regional radio stations had to keep in step with Moscow. In 1960, 'central radio broadcasting' (*i.e. Moscow Radio*) was instructed to provide transmissions of important political news and commentaries on internal and external events in good time, as well as programmes of an artistic nature.[118] Republican radio networks were ordered to arrange broadcasts in Russian as well as vernacular languages and

'to ensure the timely transmission in the vernacular of the most important news reported by the central radio; . . . to establish strict co-ordination and inter-relations between central, Republican, and *oblast* radio broadcasting and [to establish] a procedure for relaying broadcasts of news from Moscow by local radio stations; to regulate programmes relayed from central and local broadcasts by radio centres [*radiouzly*], assigning not less than half their time to artistic, chiefly musical, broadcasts and effecting the relay of all the most important news from Moscow and the Republican or *oblast* centre.'[119]

In 1962, the Central Committee expressed its continuing dissatisfaction by stating:

'Sufficiently well-defined inter-relations and co-ordination are lacking in the work of central, Republican, and *oblast* radio broadcasting and therefore important programmes from Moscow are blotted out by local broadcasts and do not reach many listeners. In recent years, the volume of local broadcasting has, unnecessarily, been greatly increased; this detracts from a radio station's strength and resources to the detriment of the quality and audibility of transmissions from Moscow.'[120]

The decree also laid down that 'in the interest of ... actively countering foreign radio propaganda', the appropriate authorities were 'to improve the reception everywhere of radio broadcasts from Moscow' and

'to organise political broadcasts from Moscow for the eastern areas of the country, taking into account the different time belts, so as to ensure that the peoples of the eastern areas are informed of all important news in the morning and evening.'[121]

The same kind of censorship applies in broadcasting as in newspapers as *Glavlit* plenipotentiaries also operate in radio stations.* Examples of *Moscow Radio's* distortions and manipulations of the news could be found daily, but two examples which occurred during visits to Moscow by the UN Secretary-General, U Thant, will suffice. On August 30, 1962, U Thant made a farewell speech in which he expressed some 'candid' statements on the theme that 'the Russian people do not fully understand the true character of the Congo problem' but 'if only they could have the means of knowing all the facets of the problem, they would certainly revise their opinion' on various pressing UN issues.[122] The full version of his broadcast was only broadcast to Britain and the USA. *Moscow Radio* put out a total bowdlerised Home Service version, omitting all potentially embarrassing passages. The Soviet people are doubly misled, therefore, when they read passages such as:

'Every year more and more prominent foreign statesmen and political figures visit the USSR. With the help of radio and television, millions of Soviet people become, in effect, direct participants in the meetings with many of these personalities and get to know the purpose of their visits and their impressions.'[123]

The reverse of this particular coin could be seen on July 30, 1964, when U Thant appeared on Moscow television. He said that the UN was faced with a financial crisis, the surmounting of which was the business of all members. A voice recording

* *See* p. 44 and Fainsod, *Smolensk under Soviet Rule,* pp. 368–9. 371.

from this speech was broadcast the same day to Africa but it omitted this passage, which could be construed as a criticism of the Soviet Union for refusing to pay its share of the UN's costs in the Congo and elsewhere.

There has been occasional criticism in Soviet sources of dubious broadcasting practices,* *e.g.* exaggeration which shades over into lying.[124] An example of the characteristic way in which people are used to publicise ready-made reports was given in a book on Marxist-Leninist ethics:

'"Always speak the truth." A little girl in the Pioneers had to learn this rule the hard way. She was asked to give a talk on the radio—to speak about the way work was done in the Pioneer camp during the summer. She gets excited, repeating the speech which she had prepared at home. The studio worker responsible for the broadcast comes in and hands the girl a previously printed text. To her feeble protest to the effect that in the camp things weren't as they were written here, he replies that that doesn't matter, the main thing is to read it out clearly and distinctly.'[125]

Yet such practices can only be encouraged by the Central Committee's insistence that 'every broadcast, every address made at the microphone, demands especially careful preparation'.[126]

Moscow Radio's foreign-language broadcasts are regarded as an extremely important weapon in waging the ideological struggle, both against the West and, more recently, against dissident Communist opinion.[127] In an announcement on October 18, 1965, *Moscow Radio* stated:

'In its broadcasts to Africa, *Radio Moscow* extensively comments on life in the Soviet Union; the African world scene; we highlight Soviet experience in Socialist construction; and present detailed information about the national liberation movement all the world over; the solidarity of progressive forces and their support of the national liberation struggle.'

In early 1965, the Soviet Union was broadcasting for 1,344 hours a week in foreign languages, considerably more than its nearest rival, Communist China (937 hours). Soviet broadcasts were in fifty-three languages (compared with the thirty-one used by China).[128] Some of these languages are obscure but politically important in the context of the Sino-Soviet dispute, *e.g.* Malayalam (the main language of Kerala, in South India)

* For a discussion of jamming, *see* p. 60.

and Quechua (spoken in parts of Latin America). In April, 1964, *Tashkent Radio* began broadcasts in Uighur, a Turkic language spoken by a national minority of the Sino-Soviet border. More generally, the dispute was the cause of a switch in emphasis in 1964. The output of broadcasts directed to Western Europe and North America by *Moscow Radio* was reduced and the South-East Asian, Chinese, and Rumanian services saw increases in output (over three hours increase in the daily broadcasts to China alone).*

Those responsible for foreign service broadcasts are, not surprisingly, highly qualified linguistically. An article on *Moscow Radio*'s British section states:

'The staff consists mainly of young Russians who have graduated from Moscow University, the Foreign Languages Institute and various other colleges. Many of them have not even been in Britain, but they have studied the language very thoroughly, and continue to study it all the time.'[129]

Two members of the section were said to be British-born. Certain Republican radios also broadcast in foreign languages (*e.g. Baku Radio* in Arabic, Persian, and Turkish as well as Azerbaidzhani). Broadcasts in Armenian, Belorussian, and Ukrainian, for instance, are also beamed to compatriots abroad by stations in the Republics concerned.

The number of television sets in the Soviet Union has risen sharply. In 1955, there were only 820,000, but towards the end of 1965, the figure had risen to more than 14 million.[130] The official view of the uses of television, as expressed in a Central Committee decree in 1960, is hardly a surprising one:

'Television, together with the Press and radio, is called upon to play an important part in educating the Soviet people in the spirit of Communist ideology and morals, of implacability towards bourgeois ideology and morals, in mobilising the workers to complete the Seven-Year Plan successfully. Television opens up great new possibilities for the daily political, cultural, and aesthetic education of the population, including those of its sections which are least covered by mass political work.'[131]

After listing a considerable number of failings, the decree went on to point out that local studios were placed in 'extremely difficult circumstances' due to the lack of a centralised system of recording worthwhile programmes on film. Some

* *See* pp. 60–61 for Soviet interference with Chinese broadcasts.

could not afford to transmit for more than a few hours a week, and this 'often at a low level'. These financial difficulties have been solved at the cost of Moscow's dominance, as in radio broadcasting:

'The "boundaries" of the programmes transmitted by Central Television are continually widening. Not so long ago the Central Studio's broadcasts could only be seen by the residents of the capital. Now its programmes are transmitted to the capitals of six Union Republics and over sixty major cities.° Radio relay communications lines make it possible to transmit television programmes not only to our country's distant cities but also across our homeland's frontiers.

. . . The prospect of television broadcasts from the capital to the shores of the Pacific Ocean lies ahead.'[132]

The highly 'political' treatment of television news can be inferred from a comment in the Union of Journalists' periodical a few years ago:

'It is strange, for instance, that "Television News" forms one of the sections of the Chief Editorial Board for Socio-Political Programmes when, by common consent, a Chief Editorial Board for "News" should have been established a long time ago.'[133]

Criticisms of Soviet television, as of other communications media, have been made by informed journalists, especially those conversant with Western practices. The well-known political commentator, Yuri Zhukov, has stated for instance:

"The impression is that we are still living in television's "middle ages". But everything can be and needs to be done in a far more lively and interesting way. In this connection there is far more imagination and inventiveness abroad.'[134]

Zhukov went on to praise the BBC and American television for their treatment of certain events. The satirical magazine *Krokodil* also ridicules the dreariness of Soviet television.[135]

The lack of freedom of expression was recently discussed by Academician Artobolevsky who said:

'In particular, one wishes that journalists would desist this year from the widely spread practice of inviting people to the television studio in order to talk from a previously prepared text which has been "checked" just in case "something might come of it." It is relevant to say that nothing good comes of it, because it bores me,

° *Tass* stated on May 5, 1965 that Moscow programmes were relayed to 100 cities.

[89]

a viewer, to hear people reading from a text . . . I just fail to understand why people working for television cling on to these texts and go in fear of living human speech.'[136]

OTHER FIELDS

There are a number of other means whereby the Soviet State has prescribed and does prescribe for its citizens what they should think and create. In music and the visual arts, for instance, the same sort of organisation operates as in literature. Left-wing (*i.e. avant-garde*) painters and sculptors are especially liable to be admonished by the party faithful.* But there is a good deal of hypocrisy in high places, as the episode described by Madame Furtseva, the Minister of Culture, shows: 'A very highly respected [*i.e.* officially approved] artist' showered typical public abuse on the non-conformist sculptor, Ernst Neizvestny, when the latter fell foul of the official arbiters. Neizvestny revealed, however, that his critic had bought one of his works from him for 12,000 roubles.[137]

The party does not only interfere with artists, writers, and journalists. All members of the intelligentsia are subjected to its control. The party's treatment of scientists is also highly shameful. As in other fields, official patronage tends to be bestowed on one scientific school or person—as has happened notoriously at various times with Trofim Lysenko, for instance. The result is that scholarly opposition becomes identified with political opposition, and exponents of the non-approved theories are silenced or discriminated against in various ways. For a world outlook which persistently claims to be 'scientific', Soviet Communism has made remarkable gaffes precisely in the realm of science.[138]

The preceding sections have examined aspects of the system of thought control. Subsequent ones will investigate the thought controllers themselves and the record of their recent actions.

* *See* final section.

SOURCES

1. *B.S.E.*, 2nd edn., Vol. 5, p. 519.
2. *Sovetskaya Pechat v Dokumentakh*, p. 210.
3. Lenin, Vol. 5, p. 10.
4. Lenin, Vol. 34, pp. 380–381.
5. *e.g.* in *Sovetskaya Pechat*, No. 4, 1965, pp. 7f. and No. 7, 1964, pp. 3–4.
6. *Sovetskaya Pechat v Tsifrakh*, p. 21.
7. *Izvestiya*, September 18, 1965.
8. There was in fact high-level opposition to the decision to abolish these *raion* newspapers: *see* the stenographic report of the 'Plenum of the Central Committee of the Communist Party of the Soviet Union', March 5–9, 1962. State Publishing House of Political Literature, 1962, pp. 104, 221, 314. For their restoration, *see Sovetskaya Rossiya*, March 17, 1965; *Sovetskaya Pechat*, No. 5, p. 49 and No. 8, 1965, pp. 3f. Over 3,000 *raion* newspapers were abolished and over 1,700 'kolkhoz-sovkhoz production board' papers started: *Pechat SSSR v 1962 Godu*, p. 17; *B.S.E. Ezhegodnik*, 1964, p. 101.
9. *KPSS v Rezolyutsiyakh*, Vol. 1, pp. 736f.
10. *See* Buzek, pp. 65f.
11. *Spravochnik Zhurnalista*, p. 59; text of decree in *Sovetskaya Pechat v Dokumentakh*, p. 258.
12. *Sovetskaya Pechat*, No. 2, 1966, p. 4.
13. *Partiinaya Zhizn*, No. 20, 1964, p. 72.
14. *Ibid.*, pp. 73.
15. *Loc. cit.* and *Sovetskaya Rossiya*, November 22, 1964.
16. *Sovetskaya Pechat*, No. 1, 1965, p. 20.
17. *Sovetskaya Rossiya*, March 17, 1965.
18. *Sovetskaya Pechat*, No. 8, 1965, pp. 1f.
19. *Sovetskaya Pechat v Dokumentakh*, pp. 301f.
20. *Sovetskaya Pechat*, No. 9, 1965, p. 52,
21. *B.S.E. Ezhegodnik*, 1965, p. 101.
22. *Spravochnik Partiinogo Rabotnika*, 1957, pp. 320, 400f; *ibid.*, 1961, pp. 468f (a revision of earlier decree).
23. *Ibid.*, 1957, p. 401.
24. *Spravochnik dlya Sekretarya Pervichnoi Partiinoi Organizatsii*, 1965, pp. 113–114.
25. Yakovlev, pp. 70f.
26. Gurevich, p. 16.
27. Yakovlev, p. 7.
28. Kutasov, *passim*.
29. *B.S.E. Ezhegodnik*, 1965, pp. 100–101.
30. *World Communications*, p. 365.
31. *Pechat SSSR v 1962 Godu*, p. 57 (by deduction).
32. *Preiskurant na Sovetskie Gazety*, p. 3.

33. 'Nikolai Gavrilov', a Soviet author writing pseudonymously in *The New Leader*, December 9, 1963, wrote: 'About a dozen people read every manuscript in the office of *Foreign Literature*, and for each reader it is a matter of prestige to find something questionable in what is submitted.'

34. Buzek, p. 247; *Sovetskaya Pechat*, No. 9, 1965, p. 2.

35. *Vestrick Moskovskogo Universitet*, Series XI (Journalism), No. 1, 1966, p. 3.

36. *See*, for example, *Soretskaya Pechat* No. 12, 1965, p. 58.

37. *Spravochnik Zhurnalista*, pp. 275f; *Organizatsiya Raboty Redaktsii Gazety*, pp. 127f.

38. *e.g. Partiinaya Zhizn*, No. 10, 1966, pp. 65–66.

39. Buzek, pp. 225f.

40. *Sovetskaya Pechat*, No. 5, 1965, p. 5, quoting the March 1965 issue of *Rabochy-Krestyansky Korrespondent*.

41. *Organizatsiya Raboty Redaktsii Gazety*, p. 65.

42. *The New Leader*, December 9, 1963. Gavrilov claimed that: '*Glavlit* does not seem to read newspapers'. This must be taken in context, however, for he had just stated that publishers (*i.e.* of books) have a 'separate department' of *Glavlit* attached. Editors are obliged to read and sign off every page. *Spravochnik Zhurnalista*, p. 250. Buzek states (p. 195) that 'final approval by *Glavlit* ... is almost always a formality'.

43. *Sovetskaya Pechat*, No. 2, 1965, p. 8. (*Agitprop* was still then named the Ideological Department.) *See* also *ibid.*, No. 6 1965, p. 11, which implies that *Agitprop* gave the newspaper *Sovetskaya Estoniya* a dressing-down.

44. *Nedelya*, January 31–February 6, 1965, p. 6; Buzek, pp. 230f.

45. Mihajlov in *Delo*, No. 1 1965, p. 92 (trans. *The New Leader*, March 29, 1965, p. 4).

46. *Sovetskaya Pechat*, No. 5, 1965, p. 6; No. 3, 1965, pp. 5, 6; No. 1, 1964, p. 52.

47. *Kommunist*, No. 10, 1965, p. 77.

48. *Sovetskaya Pechat*, No. 7, 1964, p. 10. *Organizatsiya Raboty Redaktsii Gazety*, pp. 51, 160, 161.

49. *Sovetskaya Pechat*, No. 3, 1965, p. 29.

50. *Ibid.*, No. 5, 1963, p. 10.

51. Fogelevich, pp. 153f.

52. *Za Rubezhom*, November 19–25, 1965, p. 27.

53. Fogelevich, p. 154.

54. Kruglak, p. 45.

55. *Spravochnik Zhurnalista*, p. 159.

56. *Kruglak*, pp. 187f. This section discusses *Tass* involvement in the Guzenko and Petrov cases, as well as other espionage affairs in Holland, Sweden, Turkey, etc., during and after the Second World War.

57. *Literaturnaya Rossiya,* February 19, 1965, p. 15.
58. *I.P.I. Report,* Vol. 2, No. 1, May 1953, p. 6; *Sunday Times,* November 15, 1964 (on *Tass* in London); *The Times,* January 21, 1966.
59. *Sovetskaya Pechat,* No. 2, 1964, pp. 20, 22.
60. *Za Rubezhom,* November 19–25, 1965, p. 27.
61. *Sovetskaya Pechat,* No. 2, 1964, p. 25.
62. *Za Rubezhom,* November 19–25, 1965, pp. 27–28 (details of the workings of the various editorial boards are given).
63. *Don,* No. 8, 1964, p. 88. *See also* Buzek, p. 195.
64. *Sovetskaya Pechat,* No. 2, 1964, p. 24.
65. *Ibid.,* pp. 26, 27; No. 8, 1965, pp. 2f; No. 7, 1964, p. 35; No. 1, 1964, p. 33. Goyunov's statements in: *Za Rubezhom,* November 19–25, 1965, p. 26.
66. *Sovetskaya Pechat,* No. 2, 1964, p. 27.
67. Palgunov, *Tridsat Let,* p. 267.
68. *Ibid.,* p. 299; Buzek, p. 251.
69. *Soviet News,* May 13, 1961.
70. *World Communications,* p. 367.
71. *Ibid.,* pp. 366–67; *Sovetskaya Pechat,* No. 6, 1963, p. 27.
72. *World Communications,* p. 367.
73. *Sovetskaya Pechat,* No. 3, 1965, p. 63.
74. *Ibid.,* No. 9, 1964, p. 47.
75. *Za Rubezhom,* January 8–14, 1965, pp. 23f.
76. *Loc. cit.;* *B.S.E. Ezhegodnik,* 1965, p. 24.
77. *Sovetskaya Pechat,* No. 6, 1963, p. 26.
78. *The Guardian,* December 16, 1964.
79. *The Times,* January 8, 1965.
80. *The Guardian,* September 28, 1965.
81. *Spravochnik Zhurnalista,* p. 170.
82. *Za Rubezhom,* January 8–14, 1965, pp. 23f; *Sovetskaya Pechat,* No. 9, 1964, pp. 47f; No. 2, 1965, p. 59.
83. *Ekonomicheskaya Gazeta,* February 1, 1964.
84. *Izvestiya,* July 24, 1964.
85. *Za Rubezhom,* January 8–14, 1965, p. 24.
86. *e.g.* Smirnov's letter to the London weekly, *The Economist,* on March 2, 1963, denied that a cultural 'witch-hunt' was under way in the USSR.
87. *Sovetskaya Pechat,* No. 9, 1964, p. 51; No. 7, 1963, p. 10.
88. *Ibid.,* No. 9, 1964, p. 49; No. 6, 1963, p. 27; 'Our elder and much experienced brother, *Tass*'.
89. *Ibid.,* No. 7, 1963, p. 10.
90. *B.S.E.,* 2nd edn., Vol. 27, p. 534.
91. Conquest, pp. 63f (trans. *Problemi e Realtà*).
92. *e.g.* the characteristic title of a booklet by N. Leizerov published in 1964 by the *Znanie* Publishing House in Moscow: 'The Variety of Forms and Styles in the Art of Socialist Realism.'

93. *See*, for example, the editorial footnote in *Izvestiya*, August 14, 1965, condemning certain writers' 'negative' portrayals, which was in turn attacked by *Pravda's* editor on September 9, 1965.

94. Sometimes the process goes too far: *Krokodil*, September 10, 1965, satirized the Secretary and other officials of the Khabarovsk branch of the Union of Writers who were achieving remarkable successes with their works thanks to their positions.

95. *See Swayze*, pp. 239f.

96. *Encounter*, September 1964, pp. 87, 88.

97. Boon, p. 5; *Penum Tsentralnogo Komiteta*, p. 53.

98. *Spravochnik Zhurnalista*, p. 139.

99. *Ibid.*, p. 140; *Sovetskaya Pechat v Dokumentakh*, p. 365.

100. In 1963, for instance, eight members of the editorial board of *Neva*, a Leningrad literary monthly, were sacked some months after heavy criticism of a story entitled 'Round and About' published in its issue No. 1 for 1963. One of the editors sacked was the story's author, Fedor Abramov.

101. This process has been well described by Lydia Chukhovskaya in *Literaturnaya Moskva*, Vol. II, pp. 772f. *See* also *Literaturnaya Gazeta*, January 25, 1964.

102. *Spravochnik Zhurnalista*, pp. 150–151.

103. *Kommunist*, No. 7, 1961, p. 10; *see* also *Kniga*, p. 358, where there is mention of '... nihilistic sallies against the editor, attempts ... to cast doubt on the basic principles of book-publishing. An intelligent, educated, politically literate editor, with the State's interests at heart, was and remains the author's friend, adviser, and helper and, at the same time, a demanding critic of his work and a defender of the readers' interests [sic]'.

104. *Literature and Revolution in Soviet Russia*, p. 206. *Ibid.*, pp. 202f contains useful details on the Soviet book trade which seeks to sell the kind of non-political works wanted by readers but is forced to stock 'useful' works by the authorities.

105. Quoted, *ibid.*, p. 208. *See* also *Soviet Literature in the Sixties*, pp. 157–158, 160–162.

106. Lenin, Vol. 35, p. 372.

107. Inkeles, pp. 226f.

108. *Pravda*, May 28, 1957.

109. *Spravochnik Zhurnalista*, p. 181.

110. *Loc. cit.*

111. *Partiinaya Zhizn*, No. 3, 1964, pp. 23f.

112. *Sovetskaya Pechat*, No. 8, 1963, p. 28.

113. *Loc. cit.* The State Committee also draws up a bi-annual schedule of pro-

grammes, with a view to changes. Listeners do not as yet get much say in these changes, but plans are afoot to set up an 'Institute of Public Opinion: *see Sovetskaya Pechat*, No. 2, 1965, pp. 39–40.

114. *Ibid.*, No. 12, 1962, p. 33.
115. *Partiinaya Zhizn*, No. 4, 1960, p. 29.
116. *Dvadsat Vtoroi S'ezd*, p. 215.
117. *Ibid.*, p. 216.
118. *Partiinaya Zhizn*, No. 4, 1960, pp. 29–30.
119. *Ibid.*, p. 30.
120. *Spravochnik Partiinogo Rabotnika*, 1963, p. 424.
121. *Ibid.*, p. 428.
122. Buzek, pp. 136f.
123. *Partiinaya Zhizn*, No. 16, 1964, p. 21.
124. *Sovetskaya Pechat*, No. 12, 1963, pp. 33–4.
125. *Ocherki Marksistsko-Leninskoi Etiki* by V. G. Ivanov and N. V. Rybakova, Leningrad University Publishing House, 1963, p. 226. *The Guardian*, August 20, 1965, quoted a similar story.
126. *Spravochnik Partiinogo Rabotnika*, 1963, p. 426.
127. *Ibid.*, pp. 425f. This 1962 decree stipulates, *inter alia*, that foreign broadcasts should be tailored to individual countries and groups of the population. *See* also Barghoorn, *Soviet Foreign Propaganda*, pp. 279f.
128. BBC Handbook 1966, London, 1966, pp. 96, 102.

129. *British-Soviet Friendship*, Janary 1962, p. 4. The article was 'contributed by a worker at *Moscow Radio*'.
130. *Sovetskaya Pechat*, No. 10, 1965, p. 37.
131. *Partiinaya Zhizn*, No. 4, 1960, p. 31; *see* also *Plenum Tsentralnogo Komiteta*, pp. 54, 310.
132. *Pravda*, December 4, 1964; *see* also *World Communications*, p. 368; *Sovetskaya Pechat*, No. 10, 1965, pp. 37–38.
133. *Sovetskaya Pechat*, No. 8, 1962, p. 33.
134. *Ibid.*, No. 2, 1964, p. 40.
135. *Krokodil*, September 30, 1965 (front cover); September 20, 1964, p. 12; October 10, 1964, p. 9.
136. *Sovetskaya Pechat*, No. 2, 1965, p. 34.
137. *Plenum Tsentralnogo Komiteta*, pp. 172–173.
138. *e.g.* the article by Academician Kapitsa in *Ekonomicheskaya Gazeta*, March 26, 1962, p. 10: 'Many people know what constitutes cybernetics..' But this is what was written about cybernetics on page 236 of the *Philosophical Dictionary* (published in 1954): 'Cybernetics . . . a reactionary pseudo-science ...' ... If scientists had listened to philosophers then, in 1954 ... one could say that the conquest of space, of which we are all justly proud and for which the whole world respects us, could

not have been accomplished ...'. *See* also *Voprosy Filosofii*, No. 7, 1965, p. 49, for an insight into the consequences of the change of the Party line on genetics in 1964–1965: even dialectical materialism underwent 'the most serious changes'.

V
The Party
Indoctrination System

While various State institutions provide both the negative and some of the positive means of thought control in the Soviet Union, the basic and current content of indoctrination is determined by the Communist Party itself. But it is important to realise that the thought control functions of the party are carried out at a variety of levels with a variety of instruments, from the Central Committee itself to the lowliest agitator.

Major statements of the ideological line emanate officially from the Central Committee as a whole and may be signed by one or more of its Secretaries. They are then taken up by the vast propaganda apparatus and key phrases are reiterated innumerable times. The best-known agency for spreading the word has been the Central Committee's Department of Agitation and Propaganda or *Agitprop*, also responsible for the Party's own Marxist-Leninist training system. However, *Agitprop* has suffered various vicissitudes, most recently between 1963 and 1966.

Agitprop first emerged as a separate department in the Central Committee apparatus about 1920, and in its terms of reference, formulated in a regulation dated November 1921, it was defined as the instrument through which the Central Committee was to unite and direct all the party's efforts in the realm of oral and printed propaganda and agitation.[1] It was given general responsibility for guiding the party's ideological work *inside and outside* the party's membership, and for directing the educational activities of government and other organisations. The department was divided into two in 1929, and almost eclipsed in the mid-1930s, when most of its functions were distributed among various other Central Committee departments, such as Agriculture, Industry, or Trade, each of which was made responsible for agitation and propaganda in its own sphere. In the later 1930s there were further changes, but

Agitprop gradually regained its former scope, a process which culminated in the 18th Party Congress' resolution that *Agitprop* should be reconstituted as an administration of the Central Committee. In 1948, as part of a substantial reorganisation of the Central Committee apparatus, it was renamed a department—presumably a slight demotion. It may have been at this time that *Agitprop*, hitherto consisting of about eleven 'sectors',[2] was reduced to five: propaganda, Press, science, literature, and art.[3]

Quite suddenly in 1951, two journals published under *Agitprop's* auspices—*Culture and Life* and *Party Enlightenment*—ceased publication. After Stalin's death in 1953, the Government reshuffle was reflected, without publicity, in the Party apparatus. According to scattered Press references in the 1953–57 period, the Central Committee apparatus included both an *Agitprop* Department for the Union Republics and an *Agitprop* Department for the RSFSR; mention was also made of a Department of Culture and a Department of Science, Higher Educational Establishments and Schools for the Union Republics, as well as a Department of Science, Schools, and Culture for the RSFSR.[4]

Thus culture (including literature and art), science, and education were removed from the direct competence of *Agitprop* and allotted to other autonomous Central Committee departments. The arrangement was not wholly a satisfactory one: the head of *Agitprop*, Konstantinov, speaking in 1957, said that his department 'does not influence the work of television, the cinema, etc., as we would wish it to do'.[5] It was presumably to remedy this weakness that a section was created within *Agitprop* for radio and television.[6] In addition, there was a Press section which dealt with newspapers and an editorial section responsible for periodicals.[7]

In 1963, following various other changes in ideological bodies,[*] an Ideological Department of the Central Committee was mentioned for the first time: on January 6, *Pravda* listed A. V. Romanov and V. I. Snastin as First Deputy Chairmen of the new department. (The Chairman's identity was never revealed but he was generally assumed to be Ilichev.) Romanov

---

[*] In particular, the establishment at the November, 1962, Plenum of an Ideological Commission under the chairmanship of L. Ilichev. *See* p. 141 for some of its activities.

and Snastin had previously been deputy heads of *Agitprop* under Ilichev, and this department therefore appeared to be *Agitprop's* successor, a supposition borne out by the lack of subsequent reference to the latter and the introduction of Ideological Departments in the Union Republics from the Central Committee down to *gorkom* level.[8]

However, the RSFSR (whose Party organisation differs from the other republics in that the CPSU maintains direct responsibility for it through its central Committee Bureau for the RSFSR), had two Republican Ideological Departments. One was for agriculture and was subordinate to the RSFSR Bureau for agriculture and the other, for industry, subordinated to the RSFSR Bureau for the Management of Industry and Construction. This split reflected the post-November, 1962, bifurcation of the Party and did not survive Khrushchev's exit from the political scene for long. In early 1965, there were various references once again to the Department for Propaganda and Agitation for the RSFSR of the CC, CPSU.[9] A further development was the appearance of the Department for Science and Educational Establishments for the RSFSR (followed by a Central Committee Department for Science and Educational Establishments).[10]

In the first part of 1965, the situation was clearly changing: in May, there were still references to the central Ideological Department and to the Moldavian Republican one; yet, at the same time, it transpired that a Kazakh *obkom* had an *Agitprop*. The following month came a reference to the 'Department of Agitation and Propaganda of the CC, CPSU' (*i.e.* not as before 1963, a Department for the Union-Republics), which appeared to have criticised the newspaper *Sovetskaya Estoniya*.[12] On August 1, 1965, *Pravda* referred to the head of the Department, V. I. Stepakov (whose career had previously included a spell in the Ministry of State Security[13] and who had taken over the editorship of *Izvestiya* for a time after Khrushchev's dismissal in 1964). A few days later he published his first statements in his new capacity.[14] However, on June 12, 1966, *Pravda* described Stepakov as 'Head of the Department of Propaganda of the CC, CPSU'. Similar references to the central Department followed, although for the time being, at least, there were still references to Republican *Agitprops*. The effect of this further change of name was not immediately apparent.

During 1961–62, a new network of ideological bodies spread

over the Soviet Union. It was composed of 'ideological commissions' attached to primary party organisations.* They were first introduced in Leningrad as part of the preparations for the 22nd Congress; within months there were about 400 in that city alone.[15] In due course, the Central Committee gave these 'ginger' groups a boost, urging their introduction in the Minsk region

'in order to co-ordinate the forces of all establishments and departments in the cause of the Communist education of workers, the study of pressing questions of ideological and political work . . .

As a rule, ideological commissions should be headed by the secretaries of regional, city, and district party committees.'[16]

However, many ideological commissions were allowed to disappear, though not without protest on the part of the faithful.[17] In others, there was a certain amount of reorganisation. An ideological commission in the Estonian town of Kokhtla-Yarve was reorganised in January, 1964, to include three sections (mass political, educational work, and counter-propaganda), headed by a bureau.[18]

PROPAGANDA

The classic definition of the distinction between agitation and propaganda from the early Russian Marxist Plekhanov:

'A propagandist presents many ideas to one or a few persons; an agitator presents only one or a few ideas, but he presents them to a whole mass of persons.'[19]

Propaganda is thus more a matter of education and training for the chosen few; agitation is something with a wider scope and a shorter-term impact, a means of putting the Party's policy across to the masses. The basis of indoctrination is therefore to be found in propaganda rather than in agitation.

According to the *Large Soviet Encyclopedia*, there are a number of types of propaganda 'embracing a great variety of branches of science, technology, and industrial and agricultural production'; thus party propaganda, with which we are here concerned, is only one of a list including 'anti-religious propaganda, production-technical propaganda, and agropropaganda'.[20] Party propaganda is defined as the 'oral and printed

* Not to be confused with the Ideological Commission attached to the Central Committee, whose first Chairman was Ilichev. *See* previous footnote

explanation and propagation of the ideas of Marxist-Leninism and the Communist Party...a means of ideological and political tempering of cadres, members and candidate-members of the party and of all Soviet people...'. The chief means of propaganda are the Press, oral propaganda (lectures etc.), the 'independent' study of party history and Marxist-Leninist theory, and the various institutions in the party educational system.[21]

Party propaganda is thus directed not only at party members but at 'all Soviet people' who are reached through the Press and public lectures as well as through such branches of party education as 'Universities of Marxism-Leninism'. The main effort, however, goes into the indoctrination of party members and cadres (*i.e.* party officials).

Historically, party indoctrination has altered mainly with the changing socio-educational composition of the party. The original core of intellectuals, which had formed the bulk of the party in its conspiratorial days, was swamped after the Revolution and in the 1920s by a proletarian influx. In the 1930s, however, the new class of industrial technocrats provided fresh recruits for the party with a higher educational and intellectual standard; by 1939 almost one-fifth of members and candidate-members had secondary or higher education.[22] The basic method of party education hitherto had been 'circles', *i.e.* small groups of students in factories or establishments under the guidance of a propagandist from the local Party Committee. Safe enough when it was a matter of introducing scarcely-educated workers to the ABC of Marxism, this method held dangers for the party leadership with a more sophisticated audience. In such small groups unwelcome discussions might arise, ideas be exchanged and doubts expressed. There can be no doubt that considerations of this kind prompted Stalin's statement, at the end of the period of great purges, on the need to root out the 'infatuation with the system of propaganda through study circles'.[23]

The emphasis was henceforth laid on 'independent study' or 'self-education'. The 'chief, decisive weapon' was to be the Press. The main textbook became the newly-issued *History of the CPSU (b). A Short Course*, described later as a 'new, mighty weapon of Bolshevism, an encyclopedia of basic knowledge in the sphere of Marxism-Leninism'.[24] According to the 1938 Central Committee decree which announced its publication,

the work was addressed '*in the first instance* to the directing cadres of party, Komsomol, economic and other workers,
to all party and non-party members of the intelligentsia in the
city and in the countryside'.[25] The party (and its non-party
sympathisers) were becoming more and more of an educated
élite with power in their hands, and the leaders' chief concern
was to see that this *élite* was thoroughly indoctrinated.

After Stalin's death, however, it became clear that this
cautious policy of confining the study of Marxism-Leninism to
a single textbook—moreover, one which only carried its tendentious account of party history to 1937—was self-defeating.
At the 20th Congress in 1956, Khrushchev and Suslov complained about the way in which propaganda had become 'cut
off from the practice of building Communism'.[26] These ideas
were repeated and elaborated in a Central Committee decree
in August, 1956, which, without making any radical alterations
in the propaganda system, laid down some new lines for future
action.[27] A number of innovations were introduced at this time
but the party was still by no means satisfied with its indoctrination system. In January, 1960, an important decree 'On the
Tasks of Party Propaganda under Present-day Conditions' was
passed by the Central Committee.[28] This declared that for all
its advances in recent years, 'oral and printed propaganda still
suffers from great shortcomings'.[29] The decree further emphasised that Party propaganda's chief failing was that it had not
yet overcome its lack of contact with life and 'the practice of
Communist construction', and complained that propaganda
was 'as previously, still directed primarily at members and
candidate members of the Party, the non-Party *aktiv*, and the
intelligentsia. Some groups of the population stand quite outside daily ideological and political influence.'[30]

Among the other criticisms, the point was made that the
success of propaganda work is often gauged quantitatively and
not by results; further, 'the heads of some party organisations
do not wage a persistent struggle against alien ideology, do not
give manifestations of nationalism, cosmopolitanism and an
apolitical attitude sufficient rebuff . . .'.[31]

Party propaganda, the decree emphasised, 'had to serve to
mobilise the masses' in fulfilling economic tasks (*i.e.* 'the building of Communism'). This theme, characteristic of the Khrushchev era, laid great emphasis on the importance of influencing
the world through Soviet economic achievements. Many of the

sixteen injunctions with which the decree ends merely expatiate on what has been said above: one of them, however, dwelt on the need for a 'differentiated' approach towards various sections of the population: different nationalities, women, etc.

Even this decree was apparently not specific enough, however, and in May, 1961, the Central Committee passed another: 'On Measures for the Improvement of the Selection and Training of Propaganda Cadres'.[32] The decree noted the difficulties of linking theory with practical tasks; the propagandist training machine was still mainly geared to raising the qualifications of existing propagandists rather than training the new cadres.

'As a result of the serious shortcomings in the selection and training of propaganda cadres, political studies, theoretical seminars and conferences, reports and lectures and mass propaganda undertakings are in many cases carried out formally . . . and therefore poorly assist the improvement of the economy and the education of the people in a Communist spirit.'

However, calls to improve propaganda work are still made as a matter of routine, year in, year out.[33] *Pravda* of January 13, 1965, quoted such a summons from the June, 1963, Central Committee Plenum and went on to emphasise:

'This year quite a few young propagandists who do not possess sufficient experience and have not had enough training started work. Therefore, *as never before, special attention is demanded of party committees in their work with propagandist cadres.*'

The basic way in which the party's education system functions is described below.

POLITICAL SELF-EDUCATION

The 1960 decree urged that the centre of gravity in the organisation of political education be shifted to self-education since it was 'the basic method of mastering Marxism-Leninism, fully proved in practice'.[34] It went on to indicate how times had changed: political and theoretical literature was now being published in huge editions. Only those who did not have the necessary training for 'independent work with a book' should study in circles and political schools.

Yet 'self-education' and 'independence' are not to be taken too literally:

'In political self-education, *the main attention must be concentrated on collective and seminar forms of independent study.*'[35]

A wide network of theoretical seminars was to be set up and

'the study of theoretical questions connected with practical reality and the professional interests of the audience (concrete economic problems, technical progress, Communist education, Marxist-Leninist aesthetics, the philosophical problems of biology, physics, chemistry, etc.) to be encouraged in every way.'[36]

Those studying the theory and history of the CPSU independently were to be given more help and were to be drawn more actively into practical propaganda work.[37] A Party handbook has pointed out:

'One can only find out what a Communist is studying and in which way and what help he needs, by the process of a detailed private talk [with him].'[38]

Nevertheless, party members doubtless find that they can get away with doing relatively less work through 'self-education'. It was recently complained that:

'In Kursk, for instance, there are quite a few people among the leading workers who have put themselves down as studying theory independently for years but in fact have not studied anything for a long time, rarely visit lectures and read little.'[39]

It is probably for that reason that local propagandists deprecate this method of attaining enlightenment, a fact condemned at the June, 1963, Plenum.[40]

POLITICAL SCHOOLS

In 1956, it was decided that the Political School (*politshkola*) should be a 'compulsory initial stage' for any party members who had not mastered the minimum of political knowledge contained in the standard Political Schools textbook (now called *Foundations of Political Knowledge*, a schematic work with crude illustrations).[41] It was confirmed in 1960 that the political school should be the 'initial stage in Marxist-Leninist educations'.[42]

Another attempt was made in 1965

'to create a system of political education ... [which would] solve the task of giving a sound knowledge of Marxist-Leninist theory in sequence, of [letting people receive] a *secondary political education*.'[43]

To this end, two-year Primary Political Schools and four-year Schools of the Bases of Marxism-Leninism were established.[44]

Town and district schools of the Party and economic *aktiv*, working according to the syllabus of the Higher Party Correspondence School (*Politicheskoe Samoobrazovanie* No. 2, 1966, p. 85) were another higher-level innovation.

In 1961–62, a different network of schools—Schools of Communist Labour—were established in various areas of the Soviet Union.[45] By 1964, some 80,000 of these schools were functioning[46]: most of these proved to be a convenient way of linking political and production training at a relatively low level.[47] Under Khrushchev, ideological worthiness was often equated with practical results at work.[48] The June, 1963, Plenum stressed, for instance, that

'The very heart of the ideological work of the party, Soviets, trade unions and Komsomol must consist in fostering *love and respect for socially useful labour* in every Soviet person.'[49]

Attempts were being made in 1964 to introduce a degree of standardisation in these Schools of Communist Labour as far as was practicable in the face of varied educational levels and degrees of previous participation in the party educational system. It was recommended that the size of the school be limited to 25–30 people so that individual attention could be devoted to them.[50] The suggestion was that courses were to last one to two years and consist of two or three sessions a month.[51]

STUDY CIRCLES

Various kinds of circles (*kruzhki*) meet. There are more than a million leaders of circles, seminars, and political schools in the Soviet Union; in 1964–65 over 35 million people (70 per cent of them non-party members) nominally took part in some form of Party education.*[52] The 1960 decree 'On the Tasks of Party Propaganda under Present-Day Conditions' recommended circles and theoretical seminars for the study of CPSU history, the bases of Marxism-Leninism, Marxist-Leninist philosophy, political economy, concrete economy, atheistic questions, current politics, the international situation, the world Communist movement.[53]

* Most probably these figures are inflated. The following educational year, it was stated that only nine million Communists and three million non-Party members were taking part in such education. (*Politicheskoe Samoobrazovanie*, No. 2, 1966, p. 85).

Circles studying the History of the CPSU date back to the decree announcing the publication of the *Short Course* in 1938. Only in higher level circles was material other than that work used. Although a new party history was issued in 1959, it was itself much revised in 1962.* The continual re-writing of party history in the Soviet Union must make its study unusually difficult. The first bibliographies of recommended reading for the 1964–65 political education year, for instance, were issued just before Khrushchev's fall and his works were prominently recommended; it is characteristic of the nature of the Soviet political system that his name should have been completely absent from lists issued afterwards.[54]

In view of difficulties such as these it is not surprising that some propagandists prefer caution. As an editorial in *Sovetskaya Rossiya* complained on December 29, 1964:

'... one can only describe it as absurd when, year after year, people in their study-circle study, as though from a gramophone record, one and the same material, and the propaganda of generally known truths is exalted almost to the level of virtue.'

Similarly, it has recently been said that

'... every year teaching syllabuses are changed and those subjects which have been chosen by the audience at their own wish are put aside and the same material is offered to all for study.'[55]

A complaint of a different nature is that the 'principle of voluntariness' in joining these circles is sometimes 'crudely infringed'.[56] As one writer put it:

'Quite often we watch over a Communist too much, afraid that he might be outside the system of political education. . . . A man, for instance, regularly gives political talks to the workers. . . . But we drag him into a circle, for otherwise he is "not included". . . . It is time to end distrust in questions of independent study; it is not necessary to watch over a Communist and to "enroll" him somewhere of necessity.'[57]

At least one propagandist has openly urged compulsory attendance recently, and his attitude is presumably typical of many of his colleagues who must face the same problems:

'... you won't get far with volunteers. After the working day on State farms you can only get people together for studies by compulsion or by all but ordering them. Say study periods have been

* *See* p. 151 and section on History generally.

announced. What happens? Five or six Communists turn up, and then they are late, but non-Party members are completely absent.'[58]

Sociological studies carried out in recent years and whose results have only begun to appear in print of late bear out the unpopularity of political study.[59]

A recent Party handbook reveals by inference that on occasion people have to be compelled to go to lectures:

'Some people have to be personally invited, this has to be done once or twice. You will see that a person only comes at first because the secretary of a party organisation or head of a factory shop has asked him to. But he will listen, get interested and will then come without being reminded. . . .'[60]

UNIVERSITIES OF MARXISM-LENINISM

These establishments (formerly usually qualified as Evening Universities of Marxism-Leninism) form the highest level of Party education open to the non-Party intelligentsia; they are of course also open to Party members. The universities are designed for those with higher education and practical experience. In 1961, it was decreed that their work should be reorganised so that they could train propaganda cadres for the entire Party education network.[61]

These universities existed before the war on a small scale; during the post-war years they were greatly expanded. In 1965, they had about 200,000 pupils.[62] The length of the course is two or three years.

The section on Universities of Marxism-Leninism in the 1960 decree suggested that their curricula should include:

'. . . independent work on individual plans and also in theoretical seminars on the study of individual works by the classic writers of Marxism-Leninism; individual problems of CPSU history, political economy, dialectical and historical materialism, ethics, aesthetics, atheism, the world Communist, workers' and national-liberation movements and other [problems].'[63]

There have been indications recently that not all is well with these universities as an institution. An article by the directors of two Ukrainian Universities of Marxism-Leninism stated in *Pravda* of May 26, 1965:

'The teaching plans and syllabuses of the universities have not been examined for a long time and, as a rule, copy syllabuses in higher educational establishments. We were particularly interested in why members of the historical and economic faculties lost their interest in study. The answers of many of the members boiled down to the fact that, as they said, they had studied CPSU history and political economy in technical schools and colleges and the University of Marxism-Leninism adds little to what they already knew.

'Individual Party committees . . . have in effect avoided training propagandists *via* Universities of Marxism-Leninism, do not keep a check on the students' course of study . . . facts which result in significant wastage [of students] in many instances. The weakening of daily Party attention to the Universities of Marxism-Leninism . . . has resulted in the fact that they do not occupy their due position in ideological work.'

Later it was admitted that 'a significant number of comrades who come to study in the Evening Universities of Marxism-Leninism do not graduate from them'.[64]

HOUSES AND 'CABINETS' OF POLITICAL ENLIGHTENMENT

In 1956, a decree on party education commented that many libraries attached to town and *raion* party committees were failing to be 'centres of political enlightenment' and it was therefore ordained that in the larger towns they should be converted into Houses of Political Enlightenment and in the smaller towns, in *raions* and enterprises, into Cabinets of Political Enlightenment.[65] The 1960 decree on propaganda, the main one on the subject in recent years, ordered party committees to activate these institutions and 'raise their rôle . . . in the organisation of theoretical and methodological help for those studying theory independently and for propagandists'.[66] Encouragement was to be given to non-paid helpers in Cabinets attached to major Party primary organisations. Even more stress was placed on acquiring such helpers in a decree the following year[67]: indeed the very success of the Houses and Cabinets was linked to the ability to carry this out.

The 1961 decree stated that:

'It is necessary to ensure that Houses and Cabinets of Political Enlightenment participate more actively in the selection of propagandists and the raising of their qualifications, that they generalise and popularise the best experience of Party propaganda, work out teaching and methodological aids on the basis of local material, compile lists of recommended literature, organise exhibitions and albums and carry out theoretical and methodological conferences of propagandists.'[68]

An article in 1964 on their work records that 'many Cabinets of Political Enlightenment make wide use of all kinds of technical methods: tape recorders, film-projectors, record-players—and teach propagandists, lecturers, and agitators how to use them'.[69] They also have a library with 'all the political literature necessary for current work'. The so-called 'permanently operating seminars' usually meet in these Cabinets once or twice a month.

'Here, propagandists listen to lectures and reports on the most complex theoretical problems, current questions of the Communist Party's internal and foreign policy, receive methodological instruction, exchange experience.

The article concludes with a reminder that these Cabinets are directly subordinated to the local party committee, and in particular to the head of their ideological (or, as they have since been renamed, *Agitprop*) sections.

TRAINING LEADERS

Propagandists are trained by the party in various ways: through the Universities of Marxism-Leninism; through 'permanently operating seminars' which operate at local party level and are also regarded as important for such training; and through various courses and *ad hoc* seminars.[70]

The party also ensures that people who show progress are given an 'ideological tempering' through its system of schools, higher schools, and courses. In 1919, the Communist University named after Ya. M. Sverdlov was founded and the party education network began to spread round the country. In 1931 there were fifty-five Party higher educational establishments (*komvuzy*) and the number of Institutes of Red Professorship was increased to ten.[71] The Institutes were intended to train lecturers in Marxism-Leninism and kindred subjects in HEEs. At *oblast* level and below, a network of Soviet Party Schools (*sovpartshkoly*) was started.

The pattern today is broadly similar. The Institutes of Red Professorship and the *komvuzy* have disappeared, but they have been replaced by other centres of Marxist-Leninist indoctrination. The chief of these are the CPSU Central Committee's Academy of Social Sciences and the Higher Party School in Moscow.

The Academy of Social Sciences was set up in 1946 to train 'cadres of theoretical workers for central party institutions, for Union-Republican Central Committees, and for *krai* and *oblast* committees, and also cadres of qualified teachers for scientific research institutions and for scientific periodicals'.[72] These persons include instructors for the Higher Party School as well as editors and writers for the party daily and periodical Press. The course at the Academy now lasts three years. There are classes in the following subjects: Economic Science (specialising in general problems of political economy, agricultural and industrial economy, world economy); the Bases of Scientific Communism; CPSU History; the History of Soviet Society; Philosophy (specialising in dialectical and historical materialism, criticism of contemporary bourgeois philosophy and sociology); the History of the International Communist and Workers' Movement; Literature, Art Appreciation, Journalism. The last subjects are studied in the Institute of Scientific Atheism of the Academy of Social Sciences.

According to the regulations covering 1965 entrants, candidates for admission had to be party members of at least three years' standing, under 35 years of age, with a completed higher education

'who have recommended themselves positively in leading party, State and economic work, in Press organs, in ideological organisations and in enterprises.'[73]

The appropriate Republican, *krai*, or *oblast* party committee, when recommending them, had to send various documents, including the candidate's party record and his personal file from the cadre records. Selection was by competitive examination, prior to which candidates had to submit an essay of 45–50 pages on some up-to-date aspect of their chosen subject. The written examination was of university standard and covered their own subject, the bases of Marxism-Leninism and a foreign language. A scholarship was offered to all accepted candidates.[74]

While the Academy's task is mainly to ensure that there is a supply of Marxist-Leninist theoreticians for party and other intellectually responsible positions throughout the USSR, the Higher Party School attached to the Central Committee is concerned rather with training administrators for posts lower down the scale. Its main function has been described as the

'Marxist training of leading cadres at Republican and *oblast* level from among members of the party with higher (and mainly technical) education and with adequate experience of party work.'[75] A 1962 decree on the improvement of radio and television laid down, for instance, that every year 30 to 35 editors from the radio and television network were to study at the Higher Party School in Moscow and up to 100 at Republican and inter-*oblast* Higher Party Schools.[76] Similarly, in 1961, the Higher Party School and the Academy of Social Sciences were ordered to run short courses for propagandists from party committees and the Press from Republican down to major city level. The Higher Party Schools in the Republics, *krais* and *oblasts* were to organise courses for *raion* representatives of the party and Press.[77]

An article about the work of the Higher Party School attached to the Ukrainian Central Committee mentioned the following faculties: Journalism, CPSU History, Political Economy.[78] The article stated:

'The students in the Party School thoroughly master Marxist-Leninist theory and learn how to use it creatively in the practice of Communist construction. A significant proportion of the hours of study is taken up by studying the sciences of material production. Party and Soviet construction, literature, language, the study of style . . . and other disciplines are also studied.'

The 1965 entrance regulations distinguished between those Higher Party Schools with a two-year course and the ones with a four-year course. Written examinations (at secondary school level) are taken for the latter:

'The opportunity of a fortnight's paid leave is offered in order to prepare for and take the entrance exams for the four-year Higher Party Schools and the Higher Party Correspondence School."[79]

There are also courses for foreign Communists under the auspices of the Higher Party School and other institutions in Moscow but these do not receive much publicity. A reference in a recent novel by Virta * to another little-publicised function of the Higher Party Schools is interesting: the villainous First Secretary of a fictional Central Asian Republic at one stage wished that he could get rid of a certain honest political figure by sending him off to study. Unfortunately, he had already graduated from the Higher Party School![80]

* *See* p. 143.

The Institute of Marxism-Leninism attached to the Central Committee is supposed to be the 'central party scientific institute'.[81] The Institute has changed its name more than once in its chequered history and in recent years has been subjected to heavy criticism. When it was founded in 1920, it was the Marx-Engels Institute, set up on Lenin's initiative to collect and publish the literary remains of the two founding fathers of scientific Socialism; in 1924, this Institute became the sole State repository for original documents about Marx and Engels. In 1923, a Lenin Institute was set up and soon given a similar monopoly of Leniniana. These two Institutes undertook the publication of the *Collected Works* of their eponymous heroes.

In 1931, Ryazanov, the Director of the Marx-Engels Institute, was 'unmasked as an enemy of the party' on a charge of 'having concealed from the party and the Comintern most important documents of Marx and Engels . . .'.[82] This marked the culmination of a process by which Stalin brought all Marxist and party archives under his own centralised control. In 1928, the Institute of Party History (*Istpart*) had been incorporated in the Lenin Institute, and the dispatch of Ryazanov was merely the prelude to the fusion of the Marx-Engels Institute with the Lenin Institute in November, 1931. The resultant body was named the Marx-Engels-Lenin Institute (*IMEL*).

Its history is a catalogue of unfinished tasks: the second and third editions of Lenin's works, undertaken simultaneously in 1925 (before the first edition was complete), were brought to an abrupt close in the 1930s; after 1938, when the Institute was censured by the Central Committee for the 'grossest political mistakes of a wrecking character in the appendices, notes and commentaries to several volumes of the work of Lenin',[83] it set about publishing a fourth edition (almost without notes). A Central Committee decree of January, 1957, ordained that five supplementary volumes to the fourth edition be printed but that, as the fourth edition was not sufficiently full, a 55-volume fifth edition should be completed by 1963.[84] In fact, the last volumes of the fifth edition were finally completed in 1965.[85] It is interesting to note that some faked documents used to increase Stalin's status were finally discarded in this edition.[86]

The publication of works by Marx, Engels, and Stalin has been equally subject to the vagaries of the political climate.

After Stalin's death, the Institute was renamed the Marx-Engels-Lenin-Stalin Institute. The attack on 'the cult of personality' in 1956 dictated the change to a safer label, the Institute of Marxism-Leninism.

A Central Committee decree of June, 1960, on improving the Institute's work sharply criticised the Institute's publishing activities.[87] More generally the decree complained:

'The Institute has still not become a militant scientific research centre in working out current problems of Marxist-Leninist theory. Concentrating its main attention on scientific publishing activities, the Institute hardly occupies itself with elaborating CPSU history and the most important problems of Marxist-Leninist theory connected with the practice of Communist construction in the USSR. The Institute is not waging an active struggle against anti-Marxist, reformist, and revisionist sallies abroad and publishes few works which unmask the bourgeois and social-democratic ideology of Right-wing socialist leaders and contemporary revisionists.'

The Institute's reluctance to publish material dealing with the Soviet period was noted. (It subsequently emerged that several people in the Institute of Marxism-Leninism, including its deputy director, Shatagin, had resisted de-Stalinisation, the latter doing so with all his might.[88]) The 1960 decree pointed out that the Institute 'must not only be a collector and preserver of historical documents'.[89] Among its obligations was the one 'to take part actively in the propaganda of Marxist-Leninist ideas'.

At the 1962 Historians' Conference there was much criticism of the *IML* and the low-level of the work in its branches (the Institute had been told in 1960 to improve the direction of the latter 'in a radical fashion').[90] A Ukrainian historian stated:

'The Institute of Marxism-Leninism is not now regarded as a centre of Party-historical scholarship, because it isn't one.'[91]

There are 16 *IML* branches, and in 1964 complaints were still being made about the low academic level of their staff.[92]

AGITATION

'Agitation' is defined in the *Large Soviet Encyclopedia* as political activity directed at influencing the consciousness and mood of the broad masses by means of the dissemination of certain definite ideas and slogans'.[93] It is distinguished from propaganda largely by its greater immediacy and topicality.

The means of agitation are said to include the Press, oral utterance, the radio, the cinema, and visual methods (placards diagrams, caricatures, etc.). The Press, radio, and cinema are treated elsewhere; their application to agitation differs little from their application to propaganda except in subject matter. More characteristically, however, agitation is by word of mouth.

Oral agitation may be divided into three categories: mass oral agitation *via* public addresses or by radio and television; group agitation, conducted with a few people; and individual agitation, with the agitator and his listener face to face.

Mass meetings, according to the *Encyclopedia*, 'are called when it is required to acquaint the workers quickly with the most important events in the life of the country'; they hear 'reports on current events, the international situation and the economic tasks of the particular enterprise, collective or State farm, etc. . . .'. The Party Central Committee 'has charged Party organisations with convening general meetings of the workers in all enterprises and collective farms to hear reports on current political events at least once every 1–1½ months'.[94]

These general meetings are supplemented by more frequent sessions of 'personal agitation' (in small groups or *à deux*). Indeed, according to Lenin's recommendation, quoted in the second edition of the *Encyclopedia*, mass meetings are not enough; what is needed is personal agitation—'every free day, every free hour of the conscious worker must be used for personal agitation'.[95] Such sessions are known as 'chats' (*besedy*), and regarded as the rank-and-file agitator's basic method.

'Chats' may take place anywhere, at any time. A favourite occasion is the dinner break. A recent article stated:

'Nobody is going to argue against the fact that the dinner break must and can be used for mass-cultural activities and chats on concrete questions.'[96]

Older workers who have their own living accommodation are more immune from the attentions of the agitator inside their homes except during 'campaigns'; young workers living in hostels are easily 'chatted to', however, both in the hostels, 'Red Corners', and in dormitories. An article in a recent issue of *Kommunist* (No. 10, 1965) suggested that oral agitation in homes and places of work was not enough: it should take place also in parks, stadium, *kolkhoz* markets, shops, and other places where rumours are spread. Agitation in the home and out of doors in the summer is also strongly urged in a recent Party handbook.[97]

Sometimes there is Press criticism of 'lock-ins' when workers are forced to go to a lecture or similar activity in their 'free' time by the simple expedient of locking the factory gates.[98] Even workers on the way to and from work have been exploited: agitators were let loose on suburban trains in Kharkov a few years ago, for instance.[99] Their work is not to be confused with that of the 'agit train' (*agitpoezd*) which, despite its name, is a convoy of cars stocked with literature, a film-projector, a shop, a speech-maker and a Party official, for example. These convoys visit farmers working in remote field areas.[100] Even 'agit-steamers' exist, according to the occasional reference.[101]

The reading of newspapers aloud is another function of the agitator and is combined with a group 'chat' about what has been read. The Soviet Press is frequently illustrated with carefully posed photographs of such scenes after Central Committee Plenums, etc. Agitation is also conducted under thematic headings such as 'Readings from Lenin' and 'People's Readings about Communism'.[102]

One of the agitator's main tasks is to urge improved efficiency and productivity in his chats, which usually last some 15–20 minutes.[103]

Question time with the agitator is one of the few occasions when the Soviet citizen can express a complaint. Yet he would be wise not to exceed the limit: the agitator is expected to report to the local party organisation how his 'chat' went and comment on anything of interest arising from it.[104] An official handbook contains a section headed 'How to Elucidate Pointed Questions'.[105] The main principle is that sympathy must be avoided and distractions about general improvements inserted:

'When a person experiences some sort of difficulty, it might on occasion seem to him that no solution exists, that the situation is the same everywhere and no measures are being taken. If you start expressing sympathy for such a person . . . you are only making matters worse. You must strengthen the man's confidence, demonstrate that although difficulties exist, they do not spring from anyone's ill-will but from such-and-such causes; the main thing is to demonstrate what is being done for the improvement of people's lives.'[106]

The section ends:

'One has to explain things patiently to those who really do not understand something and wish to satisfy themselves with the truth, but those who stir things up should receive a decisive rebuff.'[107]

Brief mention should also be made of visual agitation. This comprises posters, leaflets, charts of plan-fulfilment, 'boards of honour', exhibitions, graphs and pennants, etc., awarded to brigades or individual workers. A major function of such agitation is to stimulate 'Socialist competition'. Yet the general level of visual agitation is extremely low and unsophisticated.[108] A Soviet writer, E. Dorosh, included the following description in a documentary sketch:

'How very out of place and tactless now are the brightly-coloured plywood boards which were already erected last winter in the middle of the town and in the town park, with their illiterate drawings, shrill agglomeration of colours and immodest, strident captions calling on people to gather a rich harvest, produce a legendary quantity of milk and sell the State two and a half times as much as the plan demands.'[109]

The Party Statutes adopted in 1961 state that among the party member's obligations it is his duty 'to elucidate the party's policy to the masses'.[110] Agitation is one of the commonest ways for a party member to satisfy the party's expectation that he should do some party work in addition to his normal job.

Once his appointment has been confirmed, the agitator is incorporated into the *agitkollektiv*, a kind of agitators' seminar run by the primary party organisations. These were first set up in 1923. A party handbook states:

'One of the best-trained activists can head the *agitkollektiv*. But the secretary of the party organisation must personally direct the entire work of the agitators, because he knows the concrete tasks of an enterprise or *kolkhoz*, and the *raikom* or *gorkom's* instructions better than anyone else and can ensure that agitation is carried out not in an abstract manner, but closely linked to life.'[111]

Agitators are briefed as follows:

'Usually a model list of the most topical themes at a given moment is recommended to agitators every month. In thinking out such themes, the Party Bureau first asks the advice of the administration [of factories etc.], the party *aktiv*, clears up what worries workers most of all. Seminars and individual consultations are arranged for agitators on complicated questions. . . . Apart from that, the secretary and members of the Party Bureau should chat more often with agitators on the shop floor.

'But the agitator himself must display initiative in the choice of themes for chats, listening to what people are talking about, what worries them.'[112]

Additional ammunition may be found in the House or Cabinet of Political Enlightenment, under the appropriate sections of periodicals, as well as in specialised journals such as *Agitator* and *Bloknot Agitatora*. The latter, a pocket-sized magazine published in various local editions, has lost a certain amount of ground in the last few years to the former periodical, published at the centre.[113]

According to an article written in mid-1965, the turnover rate among members of *agitkollektivs* is very high: this is because party organisations themselves consider 'agitation [to be] work of minor importance, destined only for the backward strata of the population'.[114]

For all that, day-to-day pressure of direct agitation on the Soviet citizen is considerable. From time to time, the pressure is stepped up in connection with special issues, or to publicise the measures taken by various Plenums of the Central Committee. Apart from these campaigns these are the ones regularly devoted to May Day, the October Revolution and Lenin anniversaries, and to elections of the Supreme Soviets and local Soviets. For these, special arrangements are made, which include the setting-up of 'agit-points' (*agitpunkty*) in each of the sectors in which electoral districts are divided.[115] These agit-points are controlled and staffed by the local party organisations, and contribute largely to 'getting out' the vote of more than 99 per cent which is normal in Soviet elections.

SOURCES

1. *B.S.E.*, 1st edn., Vol. 1, pp. 420f.
2. Inkeles, pp. 35f.
3. Longo *et al.*, p. 58.
4. Pravda, April 21, 1953; June 28, 1953; April 21, 1956; October 23, 1956; November 23, 1956; April 10, 1957; April 24, 1957.
5. Longo *et al.*, p. 58.
6. *Ibid.*, p. 60.
7. *Loc. cit.*
8. As regards the lower levels, *Partiinaya Zhizn*, No. 24, 1963, pp. 43f gives an account of the functions of the Ideological Departments in the *kolkhoz-sovkhoz* production boards (*i.e.* the temporary successors of the rural *raions*); *ibid.*, No. 10, 1964, p. 8 refers to one attached to a *gorkom*.

9. In *Sovetskaya Pechat*, No. 2, 1965, p. 3, S. Bardin was named head of the Press, radio, and television sector of this body; *Sovetskaya Rossiya* of March 4, 1965, identified M. Khaldeev (previously head of the RSFSR Ideological Department for Industry) as head of the reinstated *Agitprop* department.

10. *Vedomosti Verkhovnogo Soveta RSFSR*, No. 10, 1965, p. 218, listed V. Mareev as head of a sector therein. (Before November 1962), a Department for Science, Schools, and Culture for the RSFSR had existed); *Pravda*, September 15, 1965.

11. *Sovetskaya Pechat*, No. 5, 1965, pp. 6, 61; *Sovetskaya Moldaviya*, May 16, 1965.

12. *Sovetskaya Pechat*, No. 6, 1965, p. 11; also *Pravda Ukrainy*, June 11, 1965.

13. *B.S.E., Ezhegodnik*, 1962, p. 616.

14. *Pravda*, August 4, 1965.

15. *Kommunist*, No. 14, 1962, pp. 59f.

16. *Spravochnik Partiinogo Rabotnika*, 1963, pp. 436–437.

17. *Zarya Vostoka*, June 11, 1963; *Politicheskoe Samoobrazovanie*, No. 5, 1964, pp. 81–82.

18. *Sovetskaya Estoniya*, May 23, 1964.

19. Quoted in Lenin, Vol. 5, p. 380.

20. *B.S.E.*, 2nd edn., Vol. 35, p. 70.

21. *Loc. cit.*

22. Fainsod, *How Russia is Ruled*, p. 231.

23. Stalin, p. 789.

24. *B.S.E.*, 1st edn., Vol. 47, p. 297.

25. *KPSS v. Rezolyutsiakh*, Vol. 3, p. 322.

26. *XX S'ezd KPSS*, Vol. 1, pp. 112, 282.

27. *Spravochnik Partiinogo Rabotnika*, 1957, pp. 346f.

28. *Ibid.*, 1961, pp. 486f.

29. *Ibid.*, 1961, p. 488.

30. *Ibid.*, 1961, p. 490.

31. *Ibid.*, 1961, p. 491.

32. *Partiinaya Zhizn*, No. 10, 1961, pp. 29f; *Politicheskaya Samoobrazovanie*, No. 5, 1965, p. 94 states that it was passed on May 5, 1961.

33. e.g. *Kommunist Sovetskoi Latvii*, No. 9, 1963, p. 9: 'How disappointing it is to see that sometimes the vital, joyful work of the political education of people is carried out formally, as a boring, bounden duty ... But one still comes across such "propagandists".'

34. *Spravochnik Partiinogo Rabotnika*, 1961, p. 499.

35. *Loc. cit.*

36. *Loc. cit.*

37. *Loc. cit.*

38. *Spravochnik Sekretarya Pervichnoi Partiinoi Organizatsii*, 1960, p. 510; *ibid.*, 1965, p. 72.

39. *Partiinaya Zhizn*, No. 16, 1965, p. 6.

40. *Plenum Tsentralnogo Komiteta*, p. 309.

41. *Spravochnik Partiinogo Rabotnika*, 1957, p. 350.

42. *Ibid.*, 1961, p. 500.
43. *Pravda*, August 4, 1965.
44. *Loc. cit.* and *Partiinaya Zhizn*, No. 16, 1965, pp. 48f.
45. *Politicheskoe Samoobrazovanie*, No. 7, 1964, p. 100.
46. *Ibid.*, No. 8, 1964, p. 79.
47. *Ibid.*, No. 7, 1964, p. 101 and No. 8, 1964, p. 79.
48. Stepakov writing in *Pravda* of August 4, 1965, inferred that such schools 'could not solve the tasks of a profound Marxist-Leninist education'. For a condemnation of 'narrow practicism' in ideological work, *see Sovetskaya Rossiya*, June 13, 1965.
49. *Plenum Tsentralnogo Komiteta*, p. 307.
50. *Politicheskoe Samoobrazovanie*, No. 8, 1964, p. 80.
51. *Ibid.*, No. 7, 1964, p. 103.
52. *Partiinaya Zhizn*, No. 10, 1965, p. 73; *Vestnik Moskovskogo Universiteta*, Series VIII (Economy and Philosophy), No. 5, 1965, p. 61.
53. *Spravochnik Partiinogo Rabotnika*, 1961, p. 500.
54. Compare *Politicheskoe Samoobrazovanie*, No. 9, 1964, pp. 28f and No. 10, 1964, pp. 47f with No. 11, pp. 34f.
55. *Partiinaya Zhizn*, No. 9, 1965, p. 50.
56. *Politicheskoe Samoobrazovanie*, No. 3, 1964, p. 108.
57. *Ibid.*, pp. 108–109.
58. *Ibid.*, No. 2, 1964, pp. 67–68.
59. *Voprosy Filosofii*, No. 4, 1965, p. 66. Only 24 industrial workers out of 136 in a small settlement took part in political study; *ibid.*, p. 79: the time spent by peasants in 'social'— *i.e.* largely political—work has decreased by over 50 per cent in the last 30 years, despite the increase in free time. The time spent on 'reading, study and self-education' has only increased by three minutes per week on average.
60. *Spravochnik Sekretarya Pervichnoi Partiinoi Organizatsii*, 1965, p. 98.
61. *Partiinaya Zhizn*, No. 10, 1961, p. 30; *Politicheskoe Samoobrazovanie*, No. 5, 1965, p. 94.
62. *Pravda*, May 26, 1965.
63. *Spravochnik Partiinogo Rabotnika*, 1961, p. 500.
64. *Politicheskoe Samoobrazovanie*, No. 9, 1965, p. 80.
65. *Spravochnik Partiinogo Rabotnika*, 1957, pp. 353–354.
66. *Ibid.*, 1961, p. 501.
67. *Partiinaya Zhizn*, No. 10, 1961, p. 32.
68. *Loc. cit.*
69. *Ibid.*, No. 6, 1964, pp. 62f.
70. *Ibid.*, No. 10, 1961, p. 31; No. 6, 1964, p. 62; *B.S.E.*, 2nd edn., Vol. 32, p. 168.
71. *Voprosy Istorii KPSS*, No. 1, 1958, pp. 112f.
72. B.S.E., 2nd edn. Vol. 1, p. 582.
73. *Kommunist*, No. 17, 1964, p. 128.
74. *Loc. cit.*
75. *Voprosy Istorii KPSS*, No. 1, 1958, pp. 120f.
76. *Spravochnik Partiinogo Rabotnika*, 1963, p. 429.

77. *Partiinaya Zhizn*, No. 10, 1961, p. 31.
78. *Sovetskaya Pechat*, No. 4, 1965, pp. 41–42.
79. *Kommunist*, No. 5, 1965, p. 128.
80. *Don*, No. 7, 1964, p. 35: 'In such cases the most suitable solution was to send the tiresome person off to study. But Ryabov . . .had graduated from the Higher Party School'.
81. *B.S.E.*, 2nd edn., Vol. 18, p. 24.
82. *Ibid.*, 1st edn., Vol. 28, pp. 548f.
83. *O Partiinoi i Sovetskoi Pechati*, p. 467.
84. *Spravochnik Partiinogo Rabotnika*, 1957, pp. 371–372.
85. *Politicheskoe Samoobrazovanie*, No. 4, 1965, p. 27.
86. *Ibid.*, p. 33.
87. *Spravochnik Partiinogo Rabotnika*, 1961, pp. 542f.
88. *Vsesoyuznoe Soveshchanie Istorikov*, pp. 271, 275.
89. *Spravochnik Partiinogo Rabotnika*, 1961, pp. 543, 544.
90. *Ibid.*, p. 545.
91. *Vsesoyuznoe Soveshchanie Istorikov*, p. 226; *see* also *ibid.*, pp. 237f, 248.
92. *Voprosy Istorii KPSS*, No. 7, 1964, p. 148.
93. *B.S.E.*, 2nd edn., Vol. 1, p. 295.
94. *Ibid.*, p. 300.
95. *Loc. cit.*
96. *Politicheskoe Samoobrazovanie*, No. 4, 1964, p. 97.
97. *Spravochnik Sekretarya Pervichnoi Partiinoi Organizatsii*, 1965, pp. 104f.
98. *Pravda*, June 7, 1963; *Turkmenskaya Iskra*, June 16, 1963; *Sovetskaya Belorussiya*, June 25, 1963.
99. *Politicheskoe Samoobrazovanie*, No. 6, 1962, pp. 99–100.
100. *Ideologicheskaya Rabota Partiinykh Organizatsii*, p. 202.
101. *Sovetskaya Pechat*, No. 5, 1964, p. 31.
102. *Politicheskoe Samoobrazovanie*, No. 6, 1964, p. 79; *ibid.*, No. 2, 1965, p. 85.
103. *Spravochnik Sekretarya Pervichnoi Partiinoi Organizatsii*, 1965, pp. 102–103.
104. *Ibid.*, 1960, pp. 520–521.
105. *Ibid.*, 1960, pp. 521f. For example of tricky questions, *see Kommunist*, No. 10, 1965, p. 47.
106. *Spravochnik Sekretarya Pervichnoi Partiinoi Organizatsii*, 1960, p. 521.
107. *Ibid.*, 1960, p. 525.
108. *See* illustrations in Kutasov, *passim*.
109. *Novy Mir*, No. 7, 1961, p. 12.
110. *Programma i Ustav KPSS*, p. 244.
111. *Spravochnik Sekretarya Pervichnoi Partiinoi Organizatsii*, 1960, pp. 503–504. *See* also *ibid.*, 1965, pp. 100f.
112. *Ibid.*, 1960, pp. 525f. and 1965, p. 103.
113. *Spravochnik Partiinogo Rabotnika*, 1961, p. 468.
114. *Kommunist*, No. 10, 1965, p. 51.
115. For the work of permanent 'agit-points', *see Spravochnik Sekretarya Pervichnoi Partiinoi Organizatsii*, 1965, pp. 103f.

VI

Thought Control in Action, 1946–66: The Party's Rôle

Previous sections of this chapter have shown how various fields of thought—economics, philosophy, psychology, literature and historiography—were subordinated early in the Plan era to the overriding demands of party and State policy; and how the media of mass communication and persuasion—Press, radio, theatre, etc.—are under the control of the State. But it is the party which controls the Soviet State. A recent party handbook has emphasised:

'As is well known, our party is the ruling one. The USSR Constitution recognised that it forms the leading core of all State and public organisations in the country.'[1]

Another section has described how the party, through its own education and indoctrination system, ensures a supply of leaders to lay down policy and of willing instruments to carry it out at lower direction levels. It remains, therefore, in this section to demonstrate how the party attempts to enforce its own control over men's minds in the Soviet Union.

A survey of Soviet thought control since the Second World War, from the first ideological whip-cracking by Andrei Zhdanov in 1946 to the hounding of Pasternak in 1958 and of intellectuals generally in 1962–63, provides examples of the party's methods.* Intellectuals, particularly writers, are a barometer of freedom.[2] The full weight of the party's ideological sanctions weighs on them, yet at the same time they are amongst the few Soviet citizens who have the opportunities to study foreign and heterodox ideas at first hand and to try and publicise them. Since the decision to do away with Stalinist methods there has therefore been a continuing battle of wits between certain members of the 'creative intelligentsia' on the

* *See* Appendix (p. 157) for the Sinyavsky and Daniel trial.

one hand, and party ideologues with allies from among the 'old guard' of writers, etc., on the other. Ilichev, Khrushchev's cultural overlord, was one of the people to point out that under the guise of fighting the remnants of Stalinism, some members of the intelligentsia went so far as to query party direction of art altogether.[3] He continued by revealing that even certain party officials (in the cultural field) were afraid of 'getting a reputation as retrogrades and conservatives'.

Massive party interference, when it does come, is dictated by a variety of immediate factors ranging from the realisation of the Hungarian revolution's implications to the obscure motivations (quite probably connected with the internal power-struggle) of Khrushchev's outbursts at the end of 1962.[4]

The war-time alliance with 'capitalist' countries forced the Soviet leaders to dilute the sour draughts of Marxism on which their subjects had been reared since the early 1930s. Once the 'second front' was opened in Western Europe, Stalin himself became generous in his praise of the West; on June 13, 1944, he said of the Normandy landings: 'One must acknowledge that the history of warfare knows no other undertakings comparable in breadth of conception, grandeur of scale and mastery of execution. ... History will mark this deed as an accomplishment of the highest order'.

Soviet history, however, was to treat this and other deeds in cavalier fashion only a few short years later. The third volume of the *History of the USSR*, published early in 1945, gave little enough attention to the Western Allies' contribution to winning the war, but was friendly in tone and did quote Stalin's appraisal of the Normandy landings, adding that the 'brilliantly executed invasion ... led to further military successes,.[5] A new edition of the same volume was issued in 1946, in which the whole account of the landing was compressed into a single brief sentence. By 1951, another version of the Normandy landing had been approved in which it was suggested that:

'England and the United States, in the course of three years of war, dragged out in every way the opening of a second front. . . . But when, after the gigantic victories of the Soviet Army, it became clear that the Soviet Union might defeat the enemy alone, occupy the territory of Germany and liberate all Western Europe ... in June, 1944, the English and American armies ... landed on the coast of Northern France.'[6]

On the whole, this interpretation remained the favoured one,[7] although brief mention was occasionally made of the 'considerable successes' achieved by Anglo-American troops.[8]

With the restoration of the old antithesis of Socialism and the USSR on the one side and capitalism and the West on the other,[9] the Soviet leaders began their carefully conceived campaign to force the whole Soviet intelligentsia to support the new Party line: the denigration of all things Western and the glorification of everything Soviet (or, by extension, Russian). This doctrinaire isolationist attitude explained such events as the hounding of the economist E. S. Varga, who had dared to imply that because nationalisation in the West was a progressive measure, the expected crisis in the capitalist countries might be staved off.

The procedure by which this post-war campaign was conducted exemplifies one of the commonest techniques of Soviet thought control; decrees are issued by the Central Committee of the CPSU, or authoritative pronouncements are made by Party leaders; their theme, including a number of key phrases, is then taken up by the whole propaganda apparatus—Press, radio, and party speakers throughout the country.

Although Stalin's ideological lieutenant, Party Secretary A. Zhdanov, died in August, 1948, his remarks at conferences set the tone for the whole of Soviet intellectual life until his master's own death in 1953. This was the period of the so-called *Zhdanovshchina*.[10] The chauvinistic side of Zhdanov's doctrine gained a new impetus, for instance, in the campaign against 'rootless cosmopolitans' which reached its peak in 1949 (and in which anti-Semitism played a very large rôle),[11] and again briefly during the trumped-up 'Doctors' Plot' in the final months before Stalin's death.

The campaign began in earnest with a Central Committee decree of August 14, 1946, entitled 'On the periodicals *Zvezda* and *Leningrad*'.[12] These Leningrad literary periodicals were reprimanded (the latter was closed down) in particular for publishing the work of Zoshchenko and Akhmatova, on whom vituperation was poured. More generally, *Leningrad* was accused of printing 'works that foster the spirit of kowtowing to the contemporary bourgeois culture of the West, a spirit which is uncharacteristic of Soviet people'.

A few days later, on August 26, another Central Committee decree was issued under the title "On the Repertoire of Dramatic Theatres and Measures for its Improvement'.[13] Once again there was a protest against 'the propaganda of reactionary bourgeois morality and ideology' and the portrayal of Soviet people 'in a freakish and caricatured form, primitive and lacking culture': this last charge had already been levelled against Zoshchenko. Playwrights, theatre critics and periodicals, and even the unwieldy play-censoring apparatus, were all issued with their ideological marching orders. Similar decrees concerning films ('On the Film *A Great Life*', September, 1946) and music ('On V. Muradeli's Opera *A Great Friendship*', February, 1948) were also passed.[14] A decade later, in 1958, the party made a rare—albeit partial—apology when it passed another decree modifying its previous abuse of certain composers (among them Shostakovich and Prokofiev); the 1948 decree was stated, nevertheless, to have played 'a positive part, on the whole, in the development of Soviet musical art'.[15] The decree on films found fault even with Eisenstein and Pudovkin, thereby demonstrating that even those relatively few Soviet artists who have gained a world reputation are not immune from censure.

PHILOSOPHY

Party control of philosophy in the Soviet Union since the war was strikingly demonstrated by the case of G. F. Aleksandrov's History of *Western European Philosophy*. Aleksandrov was an important political figure as well: since 1941, he had been head of *Agitprop* itself. This latest work, published in 1946, received a Stalin Prize. In June, 1947, however, Zhdanov condemned it in person at a conference of philosophers. 'Toothless vegetarianism' and 'professional quasi-objectivism' were among the charges hurled at Aleksandrov for the crime of civility towards his philosophical opponents in the Western world and of trying to give a rather more balanced view than was found tolerable in the Zhdanov era.[16]

The 'thaw' in philosophy, insofar as it took place, was confined to a gradual down-grading of Stalin as a theoretician,[17] some limited deprecation of previous 'sectarianism' in Soviet views on Western philosophy and science,[18] and the publication of translations of some Western philosophical works.[19] Yet in this field (as in the social sciences, such as sociology) it would be useless to expect any official Soviet efforts to seek a genuine meeting of minds: international associations are joined and co-operation allowed in a restricted tactical framework.[20]

[124]

Party dominance of the academic study of philosophy is symbolised by the fact that F. Konstantinov, an ex-head of *Agitprop* and ex-Chief editor of the Party journal *Kommunist*, has been the Director of the Academy of Sciences' Institute of Philosophy since 1962 and is the chief editor of a major *Philosophical Encyclopedia*. The history of the Party's reaction to a certain article published in *Questions of Philosophy* in January, 1962, was especially indicative. The article was unique in recent years in that it was contributed by a non-Marxist, the British philosopher, Professor F. Ayer.

Ayer's point of departure was that philosophy could not properly be described as a science as it could not be tested by experiment. A two-page editorial introduction, putting Soviet readers on their guard, preceded his 9½-page article. Following it came 16½ pages, in smaller print, of attempted refutation by one of the journal's editors. But even this defensiveness was not enough, for a few months later, *Kommunist*, in an article entitled 'Peaceful Co-existence Does Not Signify a Weakening of the Ideological Struggle', attacked *Questions of Philosophy* for its 'superficial criticism of Ayer's views,' for waging 'a very flabby academic argument' and even for making 'flattering' remarks to the effect that Ayer's 'name is widely known' and that he had 'given lectures in many of the countries of the world'.[21]

The next issue of *Questions of Philosophy* contained an abject leading article devoted to the same theme of the impossibility of ideological co-existence. After stressing the 'impermissibility of any manifestations of objectivity, of whatever kind, in criticising bourgeois philosophical conceptions',[22] the journal undertook henceforth to conduct an implacable struggle against all forms of bourgeois philosophy from existentialism, positivism, and 'Freudism' to neo-Thomism and even social democracy. The editors ended by confessing their sins in connection with the Ayer article, stating, for instance:

'The very fact that an article by a foreign scholar appears on the pages of a Soviet philosophical journal is not, of course, unusual in any way. But it is quite obvious that the publication of such items is only expedient if it serves the interest of a scientific world-outlook [*i.e.* Communism] and the strengthening of the cause of peace.'

But this particular chapter had not yet closed. In November, 1963, eight out of the 17 members of the editorial board of *Questions of Philosophy* were dropped. A note in that month's issue of the journal stated that the changes accorded with an Academy of Sciences' ruling on the periodic renewal of the staff of its journals. But several of the editors to be dropped had served for a shorter time than some of those who were retained. It is very likely that Ayer's unorthodox article was having delayed repercussions. The same issue of *Questions of Philosophy* also carried the shortened text of a report by Ilichev in which he indicated that 'a sceptical attitude was extending to philosophy in general, also including... dialectical and historical materialism'. He went on to criticise natural scientists in particular, some of whom are 'voluntarily impoverishing themselves in trying to evade the expression of a clearcut position on questions of principle concerning a world-outlook'. Others go even further in 'negating [philosophy's] significance *vis-à-vis* the natural sciences'.[23] No section of the Soviet intelligentsia is in fact better qualified than the scientists to realise the invalidity of the claim that the world-outlook of Marxism-Leninism is 'scientific'. Indeed, it is admitted that a revision of the Party line in the sciences (as happened in the field of genetics in 1964–65) may involve the revision of dialectical materialism.[24]

LITERATURE

The Zhdanov decrees * were only the culmination of a process. As early as 1943, Zoshchenko, on the basis of two instalments of his autobiography which appeared in *Oktyabr*, was denounced for presenting a view of human development incompatible with Marxist ideology, and no more was heard of this work. In 1945, the second part of Fedin's literary reminiscences, *Vanishing Petersburg*, was withdrawn from circulation and he was accused of being apolitical at a time when political ideology was helping to save the Motherland.

The repressive nature of the Zhdanov régime can be judged from two salient facts: first that many of the most distinguished Soviet writers published nothing of substance throughout the period; and, second, that many prominent writers had to rewrite their works or see them banned. Sholokhov, for example, had to re-edit certain chapters of his *And Quiet Flows the Don*.[25] Even Fadeev, chairman of the Union of Soviet Writers, was forced by Party pressure to rewrite his

* *See* pp. 123–124.

novel *The Young Guard* so as to enhance the rôle of the Communist *vis-à-vis* the local Komsomol.[26] Similarly, in 1951, Kataev had to rewrite his novel *For the Power of the Soviets*, which had been criticised on the grounds that it did not allot the organising rôle in the partisan movement to the Party.[27]

The most pernicious effect of the Zhdanov decrees, with their repeated warnings that ties of friendship must not be allowed to interfere with loyalty to the Party and State, was to revive the mistrust among the intelligentsia, which itself made it easier for the Party to retain control.[28] The animosities engendered in those years are still very much to be reckoned with. As Mikhail Romm, a well-known film director, asked in an outspoken speech in 1962: 'But is it really possible to heal the wounds, to forget what one has suffered for so many years, when one was trampled on and covered with mud?'[29]

After Stalin's death there appeared the first signs of articulate protest against the prevailing atmosphere of dogmatism and intellectual and artistic stagnation. Pomerantsev's essay *On Sincerity in Literature* (which appeared in the December, 1953, issue of *Novy Mir*) in effect questioned the prescribed criteria of 'Socialist realism' and 'Party spirit' by advocating that individual sincerity be the primary measure of creative art. Despite the very sharp criticism evoked by this essay, it was followed in February, 1954, by Zorin's play *The Guests*, in which the author was bold enough to imply that the main character, a Moscow bureaucrat involved in connivance at a 'frame-up', was a natural product of the Soviet régime which had moved away from the ideals of the Revolution and had given rise to the careerism of a new bourgeoisie.[30]

Both these works were soon denounced,[31] but the remarkable fact was that they and other unorthodox works of various kinds had in fact been published. The explanation would seem to be that the sense of disorientation following Stalin's death (like that which followed his denunciation by Khrushchev in 1956) was shared by writers, editors and censors alike, who were given no clear indication of the limits to be set on the new spirit of criticism.

Ehrenburg's *The Thaw*, first published in the May, 1954, issue of *Znamya*, was a further indictment of the conformist requirements of the Soviet social system. The title of the novel has since been widely applied to this and subsequent periods of relative relaxation in the party's control of intellectuals.

Changes in the political life of the country—the down-grading of the Secret Police, a franker approach to economic shortcomings, etc.—had a corresponding influence on literary activity, creating a highly complex situation. Works that had been previously banned were reprinted, writers who had been silent for years now reappeared in print (Akhmatova and Zoshchenko among them), while the subject matter of creative writing was slowly broadened to include topics rarely, if ever, mentioned in the past (*e.g.* Korneichuk's *Wings* dealt with the abuses of the Secret Police under Beria, and Stein's *Personal File* with intrigue in the party apparatus). In April, 1954, a number of poems from the epilogue of Pasternak's *Dr. Zhivago* were published, and in a foreword the author announced that he proposed to finish the novel itself in the summer of the same year.[32]

The party was, however, uneasy at the way events were shaping and official criticism of certain writers and their works was accompanied by changes in the staffs of the literary journals which had published them.[33]

There was much animated and even acrimonious discussion at the Second Writers' Congress held in December, 1954. Although its formal resolutions marked no advance in the official attitude towards the writers' social functions and towards the limits of creative freedom, it did not halt the process of rehabilitation which continued into 1955. Decisions were taken to republish writers long in disfavour, such as Babel, Tsvetaeva, and others. Yet the party Press continued to remind its readers of the validity of the notorious decrees of 1946–48.[34]

One literary theme which merits special mention in the context of thought control is rural life. Ever since collectivisation, agriculture has been the Achilles' heel of the Soviet economy. The party authorities have been—and still are—particularly sensitive to any tendency on the part of writers to reveal the truth about primitive conditions in the farms and the continuance of age-old peasant attitudes and customs.

During 1955, however, a significant change in the permitted literary approach to the subject of *kolkhoz* life appears to have occurred. While remaining within the prescribed ideological limits, a number of writers, of whom the most prominent was Ovechkin, began to infuse greater realism into their depiction of rural life. They were tolerated only as long as the 'negative' features they described were ascribed to individual human causes and not to the Soviet system. More fundamental treatment of the agricultural problem still remained dangerous: Panferov had been strongly attacked for his novel *Mother Volga* which had drawn a largely tragic picture of the once fertile lands of the Volga, now derelict because of administrative failures.[35]

A similar fate befell Pogodin, whose play *We Three Went to the Virgin Lands* was first staged in November, 1955. Based largely on first-hand material, it dealt with the hardships and privations endured by young people who had responded to the call for volunteers in 1954; it paid scant attention to the 'heroic' aspects of Khrushchev's Virgin Lands campaign then in full swing. Despite early enthusiastic reviews,[36] it was soon condemned by *Pravda* as a 'serious failure'.[37] The theatre which produced it was reprimanded, as were the critics who had praised it and the body responsible for showing the play on television. This was the first time since Stalin's death that *Pravda* had denounced an individual work. Pogodin undertook to rewrite the play.[38] Even Sholokhov had to recast certain chapters of the second volume of his *Virgin Soil Upturned*.[39]

Over the years the names of certain writers dealing with rural themes have recurred. Alexandr Yashin's celebrated story *The Levers* revealed the gulf between party officials and the farmers themselves (the latter being mere 'levers' of the party in the eyes of the former).[40] Yashin was severely censured and apparently did not appear in print again until 1962, when *Novy Mir* published a sketch of his entitled *Vologda Wedding*.[41] This reported ancient, even atavistic, marriage rites still current and, inevitably, attracted criticism.

Another case in point is the writer F. Abramov, who had found himself bracketed with Pomerantsev[42] as a result of his debunking article on *kolkhoz* fiction, published in *Novy Mir*, in April, 1954. A striking story by Abramov, *Round and About*,[43] appeared in the Leningrad literary journal, *Neva*, in January, 1963: some months later, after party criticism, Abramov and several other editors of *Neva* were dropped from its editorial board.[44] The story described a day in the life of the chairman of a *kolkhoz* (ironically called the *New Life*, in the village of Bogatka, a word which implies 'rich'). The chairman was the 13th to occupy this post since the war. The farmers' lack of interest in the collective economy, as opposed to their own private farming and activities 'on the side', was made clear throughout. Among those who criticised (or were made to criticise) the story were the inhabitants of a village which was apparently Abramov's model.[45] After a similar letter had been published[46] about another work on a rural theme (E. Dorosh's *Village Diary*), *Novy Mir's* editor, Tvardovsky, launched a vigorous counter attack against this

'method of organising "statements from the horse's mouth", when a hastily prepared "document" is equipped with the signatures of people who are often good but do not know that they have been drawn into an unworthy affair. These facts are eloquent of how difficult it is for the sad heritage of years now past to die out in literary life as well; at that time, various highly damaging habits of falsifying and distorting the truth of life developed and took root, giving rise to distrust of our printed word among people.'[47]

The year 1956 marked a climacteric in the ebb and flow of cultural control and relaxation in the Soviet Union. In February, a group of Moscow writers were allowed to publish the first volume of their own almanack, *Literaturnaya Moskva (Literary Moscow)*. The contributions were exclusively literary. While they contained nothing obviously revisionist, neither was the accent on ideology. This collection, although the most successful, was only one of a whole number of literary collections and almanacks published around this time.

Khrushchev's revelations at the 20th Party Congress had a violent impact on intellectual activities, particularly on literature, and were genuinely regarded by many writers as an invitation to greater freedom of expression. The disclosures had, moreover, impaired the authority of the literary bureaucrats so that they temporarily lost control of the situation. Poems, stories and novels now began for the first time to contain allusions to the horrors of the Stalin period, to arrests, interrogations and prison camps. This process was to continue with increasing momentum, but that it was by no means identical with freedom of expression in general became apparent when Solzhenitsyn's *One Day in the Life of Ivan Denisovich* was immediately followed by Khrushchev's outbursts against ideological lapses in the arts (*see* below).

The parade of literary non-conformity in 1956 was led by *Novy Mir*, which two years earlier had undergone a change of editorship designed to ensure its doctrinal purity. Of the unorthodox works published by the journal, the greatest *succès de scandale* was attained by Dudintsev's novel *Not By Bread*

Alone (August–October) with its unflattering depictions of bureaucrats.

The demand for greater creative freedom was taken up by some literary critics, the campaign reaching its climax in an article published in *Questions of Philosophy* by B. Nazarov and O. Gridneva.[48] Official reaction was sharp[49] and in its next issue the editors confessed to a serious error in printing the article and warned their readers that intellectual dissensions within the Soviet Union were being exploited by 'international reaction.'

By late 1956, the literary dispute had become caught in the backwash of the political crisis in Eastern Europe. Both were the direct result of the de-Stalinisation campaign, and both were solved by reversions to harsh repression. The official counter-attack was most vigorous. It began in October over Dudintsev's novel and Granin's sketch, *Personal Opinion*[50]; any literary material which smacked of non-conformity no longer found its way into print. The campaign reached its peak after the publication of the second volume of *Literary Moscow* which appeared, by some strange lapse of the censorship or, more probably, through the inertia of the bureaucratic machine (it had been passed for publication in November) in January, 1957. Its contents were more unorthodox than those of the first volume and were assailed in the Party Press, its editors being charged with 'revisionism' and with aiding bourgeois detractors of the Soviet régime. At the same time, plenums of Republican Writers' Unions were convened and urged to condemn various harmful trends.

The ground was now ready for Khrushchev's personal intervention. In later years, similar meetings were almost invariably described as 'traditional', but the 'tradition' only stretched as far back as the three occasions in the spring and summer of 1957 when he lectured groups of writers and artists on their duties in Soviet society. He attacked Margarita Aliger and Dudintsev by name,[51] and referred obliquely to the continuing validity of the Zhdanov decrees.[52] He alluded to the 'lesson of the Hungarian events, when the counter-revolution used certain writers for its own filthy aims'.[53] He is reported to have gone further at the May 19 meeting, stating in an aside that unlike the Hungarian authorities, he would have no hesitation in shooting a couple of leading writers.

In due course, the dissident writers recanted; one of the last to do so was Margarita Aliger whom Khrushchev had reduced to tears at the May 19 meeting and who had been under attack for her own poetical works and for her co-editorship of *Literary Moscow*.[54] Preparations now went ahead for the third Writers' Congress, which was, however, postponed for several months.[55] This was not surprising in view of the unsettling effect on Soviet literary circles of the award of the Nobel Prize to Boris Pasternak in October, 1958. The treatment of Pasternak vividly demonstrated to the outside world how creative freedom is openly sacrificed to political ends in the Soviet Union. Abuse which would have been outrageous when publicly applied to a lesser figure descended on him.[56] Yet the meeting at which Pasternak's 'treacherous behaviour' had been 'unanimously' condemned and he himself expelled from the Union of Writers, was also stated to have been the scene of 'heated discussion'.[57]

Khrushchev's speech at the writers' congress—a well-drilled affair which maintained a polite fiction of 'unanimity'—reflected the victory he felt he had won. He could now afford a reasonable display of clemency. Those who had recanted their 're-visionist views' should be helped to re-embark on the right path. There should be no recrimination but neither should past events be forgotten. It was the party who had the right to uncover failings and not those writers who only looked at the dark side of Soviet life. An important theme was his (*i.e.* the party's) disingenuous refusal to run writers' affairs for them, to decide what to print, etc. This was a task for writers, and, in particular, for literary critics.[58] This theme of self-management (which was to recur in the party Press in subsequent years[59]) was eagerly seized on, for their own purposes, by the unions themselves. These have become the main battlefield in the struggle between the old guard of writers, unrepentant of their Stalinist past, and many younger writers abetted by such liberal spirits of the older generation as Ehrenburg, Paustovsky, Borshchagovsky and Shchipachev. To take but one example, elections to the board of the important Moscow section of the RSFSR Writers' Union (otherwise known as the Moscow Writers' Organisation) have been hotly contested by the two opposed groups in recent years.[60]

Indeed, the change which took place in the leadership of the USSR Union of Writers on the day after the Third Writers' Congress ended in May, 1959, seemed a good augury. A. Surkov, prominent in the hounding of Pasternak, was replaced as First Secretary by K. Fedin, a much more respected figure. A period of relative stability followed, although differences lay not far below the surface. V. Kochetov, one of the most notorious 'retrogrades' went as far as to refer to the opposing 'sides'.[61] The most important literary newspapers were becoming identified with these factions. *Literature and Life*, the organ of the RSFSR Union of Writers (established in December, 1958, as a counterweight to the USSR Union) on the whole took a hard doctrinaire attitude, while the *Literary Gazette* (organ of the USSR Union of Writers) tended to adopt a more moderate posture. Ironically, it had until recently been edited by Kochetov who had retired, ostensibly because of ill-health. The incipient feud between the two newspapers came to a head following the publication in *Literary Gazette* on September 19, 1961, of Evtushenko's celebrated poem, *Baby Yar*, which attacked anti-Semitism both as a historical phenomenon and, more particularly, as one still extant in the Russia of today. This topic is a particularly sensitive one, for ideological reasons (such negative phenomena are not supposed to exist in Communist societies); it also bears a reminder of Stalin's 'anti-cosmopolitan' campaign. Among writers it is the more 'Stalinist' who also tend to be the chauvinistic ones, and it was two of the latter who hastened to the attack in *Literature and Life*.[62]

In July, 1960, there was another meeting between Party and Government leaders and representatives of different spheres of cultural life, although it was not until May, 1961, that a 'shortened' version of Khrushchev's speech was published in *Kommunist*. The tone was largely one of complacency. Artists, Khrushchev said, 'accept the Party's ideas as their own ideas'. Yet he went on to say that it was pointless to try to conceal the fact that some writers, film-producers, etc., resented the advice of their colleagues and saw it as being restrictive.[63]

In August, 1960, *Novy Mir* began the publication of Ehrenburg's memoirs, *People, Years and Life*.[64] This was an undertaking of more than literary importance. Ehrenburg made no secret of his love for 'formalist' art, *i.e.* 'modern' art as opposed to the didactic clichés of Socialist Realism. His travels before the war—to France and Spain in particular—had brought him into contact with many artists about whom the Soviet public knew little. The writer was to be criticised for the views on art expressed in his memoirs[65]; more violent attacks were launched at the end of 1962, however, because of his incursion into forbidden political territory. Ehrenburg had openly stated that in the 1930s he, and the Soviet people at large, had been forced to remain silent in the prevailing circumstances, although aware of the crimes which were being committed.[66] This assertion was, politically, most embarrassing to the top Party leadership. Khrushchev tried to divest himself of guilt, claiming that 'the leading cadres of the Party' did not know 'that absolutely innocent people were being arrested ... Stalin's abuses of powers and the facts of his arbitrary rule only became known to us after his death and the exposure of Beria'.[67] In an attempt to discredit Ehrenburg, comments were made about the latter's own sycophantic past. Khrushchev implied that he was a coward to have kept 'silent' when Sholokhov and 'other courageous Communists' had complained about injustices.[68] Moreover, unlike others, he had not been arrested[69]: the implication was that he had managed to trim his sails to the wind.

Early in 1961, Kochetov returned to a position of influence, becoming chief editor of the literary journal *Oktyabr*. Later in the year his new novel, *The Obkom Secretary* (*i.e.* Secretary of the regional Party committee), was serialised in *Zvezda*. This work disgusted liberal writers for the way in which its hero, Denisov, shirked coming to terms with Stalin's crimes[70]; it also contained a caricature of Evtushenko.

In October, 1961, the 22nd CPSU Congress was held and the new party programme confirmed. The latter document contained a section characteristically entitled 'The Enhancement of the Educational Rôle of Literature and Art'[71] which was on entirely orthodox lines and concluded[72]:

'The Communist Party sees to the correct tendency in the development of literature and art ... aiding public organisations and creative unions ... in their activities.'

A few telling points of literary interest were made at the congress. Tvardovsky pointed out how impossible it would be to share a railway wagon to Vladivostok with a 'model' (*i.e.* 'positive') hero[73] and Sholokhov derided the figure previously given by the Minister of Culture, Madame Furtseva, of the number of plays devoted to contemporary (*i.e.* propagandist) themes. He asked how many would survive—perhaps 20 or 30, if not less, out of the 780 produced so far that year.[74] A leading politico-military figure, Golikov, complained about 'elements of pacifism' which had appeared in some works,[75] and similar complaints have been made many times since the congress.

In December, 1961, after the congress ended, a large-scale ideological conference was held in the Kremlin. Criticism was levelled at the writers V. Aksenov and V. Rozov whose preferred theme is Soviet youth—but not the cardboard figures usually featured in Soviet fiction. Some of Aksenov's heroes were said to 'flirt with cheap scepticism and explain themselves in hideous slang'.[76] Party dislike of writers who portrayed youthful scepticism broadened into heavy attacks on those who dared suggest that the younger generation saw itself as differing from its elders. The implication here was that young people despised their fathers for their mute acceptance of Stalinism. Soviet officials insisted that the 'problem of the generations' was an artificial one invented by the West, but occasional admissions that it existed were made.[77] That the theme had a basis in actuality despite disclaimers from Khrushchev[78] and lesser spokesmen was further suggested by its popularity, particularly among dramatists, who in due course attracted the bulk of the criticism.[79]

Throughout 1962, young writers were, in fact, encouraged to view themselves as being in a category apart.[80] A Conference of Young Writers was due to take place in the autumn (although it was repeatedly postponed and only held finally in May, 1963) and there was a great deal of advance publicity. In particular, 32 young writers answered a questionnaire in *Questions of Literature* in September. Many of their answers emphasised the importance of 'truth' and were appropriately forward-looking. The *avant-garde* poet, A. Voznesensky, said that Pasternak was the only man of letters to have influenced him. Others also cited Pasternak, as well as Babel, Hemingway and other writers not identified with Socialist Realism.

The sparring between 'Left-wing' artists and writers of the Evtushenko and Voznesensky type against the Gribachevs and Kochetovs would probably not have been possible had an overall policy of literary de-Stalinisation not been decreed at the very top. During 1962, writers had inserted episodes concerned with the evils of the personality cult into their works almost as a matter of routine. Some efforts stood out, however: Yury Bondarev's novel *Silence*[81] contained an extremely graphic account of the arrest of a loyal Communist; the novel's protagonist, a war-hero unjustly expelled from the Party and the institute in which he was studying, pointedly asked himself how the Party could include some of the villains who figure in the work. (A film which was later made from this work toned down certain scenes and ended on much more of an up-beat note.)

The first major anti-Stalinist sensation of the year, however, was Evtushenko's poem, *Stalin's Heirs*. The author has stated that 'editors were afraid to publish' until it was sent to Khrushchev[82]: it appeared in *Pravda* on October 21, 1962.[83] The poem implied that 'Stalin's heirs' were still alive. Open reference was made to the Albanian leader, Hoxha (still standing in for the Chinese leadership at that stage of the Sino-Soviet dispute). But Evtushenko also referred to Stalinists within the Soviet Union, although it is a subject for debate whether he was referring to a specific Soviet leader, Kozlov.[84]

Several other anti-Stalin works also appeared at this time,[85] but everything hitherto published on these themes was eclipsed by A. Solzhenitsyn's story *One Day in the Life of Ivan Denisovich* (*Novy Mir No. 11*, 1962.).[86] It is almost certain that Khrushchev personally gave instructions to publish this work in the face of high-level opposition.[87] His intention was doubtless to demonstrate once again—albeit in a controlled manner —that the party condemned the 'excesses' of its Stalinist past. His own identification of this and other de-Stalinising works with 'party positions'[88] denotes an expectation that credit for them would rub off on to the party, which allowed their publication, and on to him personally. (Khrushchev went out of his way to act as Solzhenitsyn's patron at a meeting on December 17, 1962.)[89] Biographical details published about Solzhenitsyn stated that he had himself been unjustly detained for eight years in a forced-labour camp.

It can only be assumed that Khrushchev's eagerness to be associated with this anti-Stalinist bombshell blinded him to its very real unsuitability as a party-minded treatment of life in a forced-labour camp. The reactionary critics certainly did not miss the point although the brunt of their attack only came later, after Solzhenitsyn had published more stories. These only emphasised what had been obscured by the emotion surrounding the publication of *One Day . . .*: his heroes had a near-religious resignation in the face of injustice which was incompatible with 'positive heroism'. Whatever they were inspired by, it was certainly not the ideals of Communism.[90]

The liberal intelligentsia had reason to feel high-spirited in November, 1962, and therefore the atmosphere was reminiscent of the great 'thaw' of early 1956. Quite suddenly, however, the tide turned for reasons which have not been fully elucidated, although internal Party politics probably played some part.[91] The most obvious causes of the initial outburst were Khrushchev's own Philistinism and his annoyance with senders of petitions for greater intellectual freedom.[92]

In the months to follow, the liberals' many enemies seized every opportunity to smear and pillory them. To a large extent, therefore, the campaign snowballed. The level to which criticism descended was exemplified by the Leningrad Party leader who, in addition to assailing heterodox intellectuals, pointed out that shop windows and theatrical posters were not free from the baneful influence of abstract art and formalism.[93]

On December 1, 1962, Khrushchev visited the Manège exhibition hall where two separate exhibitions were housed. The first, 'Thirty Years of Moscow Art', had been open to the public for some weeks. Among the works on view were some which did not accord with the canons of Socialist Realism although it is interesting to note that most of them had been praised before the top-level visit.[94] A closed exhibition of much more advanced works had also been hastily assembled. Khrushchev's displeasure at what he saw was made clear enough in *Pravda*[95] although he himself used the crudest abuse.[96] On December 17, in an atmosphere of mounting tension, a meeting was held between party leaders and several hundred intellectuals. Khrushchev's speech on that occasion was never published,[97] yet a fairly full account of how the proceedings were deliberately staged was published later.[98] One room, for instance, was specially set aside for the works of 'home-grown abstract painters' calculated to horrify delegates from the provinces. Neizvestny's works were brought in at the appropriate moment as 'proof', at Khrushchev's request. Ehrenburg was in the very thick of the criticism. The notorious reactionary, Gribachev, 'unmasked the anti-people idea of the peaceful co-existence of the two ideologies proposed by I. Ehrenburg as an attempt at internal sabotage'.[99] This was a reference to the letter advocating ' "peaceful co-existence" of *all* trends in art' which, according to Ilichev, had been sent to the Central Committee and then recalled by the signatories.[100] Later it became known that these included A. Surkov[101] which must have been a blow to the authorities, however well aware they must have been of Surkov's opportunism. Ilichev claimed that this plea was 'objectively' equivalent to a plea for peaceful co-existence in ideology. Khrushchev had in fact been even more uncompromising in his unpublished speech a few days earlier, for he had[102]

'emphasised in the most categorical way that "peaceful co-existence in the sphere of ideology is treachery to Marxism-Leninism . . .".'

Although errant painters had been the first targets, before long writers, musicians, critics, and other intellectuals all found themselves assailed in the Press and at meetings throughout the USSR. *Izvestiya* on January 20, 1963, criticised the well-known writer V. Nekrasov who had written reports on his visits to Italy and the US.[103] These had been remarkably frank by Soviet standards, and among the sensitive topics Nekrasov dwelt on were Soviet ignorance of Western culture. (He recalled in shame how some leading Soviet writers had had to admit a few years previously that they had never heard of Kafka.) The tiresome supervision of his group of visitors to the US by a perpetually frightened Soviet security official was described as well as the stereotyped reaction of one of his group to the American scene. (The latter had gone out of his way to try and find slums and had painted a ludicrously black picture on his return.) Nekrasov, on the other hand, greeted works of art and modern buildings with enthusiasm.

Izvestiya's unsigned (*i.e.* editorial) attack ended by stating that Nekrasov's incorrect generalisations and parallels tended *inter alia* to 'bourgeois objectivity', a grave heresy to be levelled at a Communist. Despite heavy criticism by Khrushchev and leading Ukrainian Party officials,[104] Nekrasov refused to recant fully.[105] As late as the June, 1963, Plenum, an angry Khrushchev suggested that he be thrown out of the Party.[106]

Other leading intellectuals were also courageously refusing to recant, or doing so in ways equivocal enough to make fools of the party (*e.g.* Neizvestny and Voznesensky).[107] In the outlying Republics, the cultural purge often went to the other extreme and had 'national narrow-mindedness' as one of its chief targets[108] rather than foreign influences. The party did not have everything its own way, however: *Izvestiya* published a report[109] about an architect who 'started to fling dirt at recognised masters of our Soviet art, praising the "masterpieces" of

Neizvestny, abstract art and abstract artists in every way' at a public meeting in the capital of Kazakhstan. Presiding officials had even let him have his say. As the campaign progressed, an air of 'wait and see' materialised.[110] This was not surprising because the counter-measures suggested and those eventually initiated were feeble in the context of the furious verbal and published onslaughts. Liberals were encouraged by an interview (published in *Pravda* on May 12, 1963) which Tvardovsky had granted an American newspaper correspondent.[111] It had been rumoured for some time that Tvardovsky was about to be dismissed from the editorship of *Novy Mir*; he had openly been called upon to confess his sins in public.[112] Instead, what *Pravda* now published was nothing short of a discreet defence of *Novy Mir's* publishing policy, and the disclosure that works by some of the most criticised writers—including Nekrasov—would be appearing in the journal later that year. Such statements must have received high-level clearance. A week later, a *Pravda* editorial urged boldness and independence and stated that the party saw 'no need to watch over every step' by intellectuals or to explain in detail how they were to create works of art.

The June Plenum, devoted to ideology, accentuated the note of bathos. Khrushchev's ominous reference to Taras Bulba's slaughter of his own son when the latter went over to the enemy[113] was empty rhetoric. The six-month storm, in fact, had few institutional or indeed other obvious results to show for itself. The most widely canvassed suggestion, that a single artistic union be formed (*i.e.* one which the then triumphant conservatives would dominate) was shelved.[114] A sorry tale was told by Adzhubei about how the Moscow Party Committee tried to assign Communist writers to various party organisations, including those in large factories, the intention doubtless being to get writers 'closer to life'. A spot-check had revealed that only one writer had approached such an organisation, the party committee of a watch factory, and he had wanted his watch repaired![115]

Nevertheless, there was a tightening of controls within the unions. Unreliable sub-sections disappeared or had their teeth drawn.[116] Some of the writers who had been criticised had foreign engagements cancelled[117]; (frank interviews given abroad by Aksenov, Voznesensky, and Evtushenko, for instance, had given rise to some of the worst onslaughts of the preceding months). More generally, one of the periodic 'vigilance' campaigns was launched against the West,[118] coinciding with uncompromising official denouncements of Western cultural influences.

Yet even as outside influences fanned the flames of this controversy, they also helped to put them out. Foreign Communist reactions were strong, especially in Western European countries where Philistine and even xenophobic Soviet attitudes proved an embarrassment to the local Communist Parties in their struggle against democratic ones for political power. This was particularly the case in Italy. When *Pravda* published Togliatti's final memorandum over a year later,[119] Russians could read for themselves suggestions that what was needed was a 'dialogue' and 'continual discussions' with representatives of different cultural tendencies. Togliatti all but spelled out that the Soviet Union was too dogmatic in its attitude and was failing in the task of unmasking 'the genuine enemies' of art. At the time, however, comments by John Gollan of the British CP, for instance, on the theme that 'the Communist Party does not regard it as its function to issue directives to our artists and scientists on their artistic and scientific work'[120] naturally did not feature in a *Pravda* summary.[121] Such strongly voiced sentiments, presumably urged even more in private than in public, must have had some effect on the Soviet leadership—particularly as it was trying to rally support against 'Stalinist' China.

The Soviet Union was also deeply committed to its own efforts at making friends and influencing people on an international scale. In July, 1963, the Third International Film Festival was held in Moscow, and after extraordinary behind-the-scenes activities the jury—six non-Communists and nine from bloc countries—chose Fellini's highly subjective 8½ for the highest award.[122] The next month, a hundred writers from East and West met in Leningrad under the auspices of COMES (the Community of European Writers, a body dominated by the Left) and UNESCO.[123] Some of the Soviet delegates proceeded to re-fight a battle long since won in the world of letters by assailing Proust, Joyce, and Kafka.[124] Ehrenburg, who to general surprise was allowed to speak at the conference, referred sharply to such criticism of foreign authors. 'We cannot argue here about books that are known only to a few writers of our country', he said.[125]

After the conference, several of the writers travelled to Khrushchev's Black Sea villa for a rather baffling audience.[126]

[140]

This ended on a note of inconsistency which seemed appropriate in view of the zig-zags of recent cultural policy. Khrushchev asked Tvardovsky to read his long verse work, *Terkin in the Other World*, which had been circulating in manuscript for years, in accordance with the old Russian tradition involving politically sensitive works. Its subsequent publication in *Izvestiya*[127] merely emphasized the signal already given by Tvardovsky in his May interview. The worst was over for the time being.

Tvardovsky's verse attack on Stalinism contained the assertion that Stalin was still 'partly' alive—and liberal intellectuals needed no reminder of this. The 'drought' which was to affect Soviet literary life after the events of 1963 was forecast in a remarkably bold poem by Bella Akhmadulina, Evtushenko's ex-wife and one of the best of the young Soviet poets.[128] The extract which found its way into print despite its plain references ended with the words:

'The weather forecasters, plunged into fear, promised that there'd be no rain ever again.'

This pessimism was justified initially. The first works published by Evtushenko and Voznesensky since they had got into trouble were rather more conformist than had been their wont in the recent past.[129] Ilichev's Ideological Commission was very active in the winter of 1963–64, meeting several times to discuss matters ranging from the theatre and the work of the Moscow film studio to illustrations in children's books. The playwright, A. Stein, was heavily criticised in *Pravda* of July 12, 1964, for his work *Between the Downpours*, published earlier in the year,[130] dealing with the Kronstadt rebellion of 1921. *Pravda* attacked Stein on grounds of interpretation and for sins of omission, stating that 'serious work' had to be done on the play as a 'matter of honour' for its author. In due course Stein stated that he was following this advice,[131] and a year later *Pravda* praised the revised version.[132]

Polemics continued to rage in the pages of literary publications, particularly over *Terkin in the Other World* and Solzhenitsyn's works which provided a banner for one faction and a target for another.[133] This was despite injunctions against factionalism by Ilichev and Khrushchev. Several instances of individuals holding out strongly against criticism[134] were mentioned in public, providing proof of the Party's inability to maintain conformity.

One ugly sanction was preserved from earlier times, however—the incarceration of hostile intellectuals in lunatic asylums. Several cases of this kind have come to light in recent years, and they usually followed the dispatch of manuscripts abroad. After the Pasternak case in 1958, the Central Committee apparently forbade writers to publish material abroad without prior clearance within the Soviet Union.[135] In any case, for one person to hand a manuscript over to another for the purpose of delivering it abroad appears to contravene Soviet postal and customs regulations.[136] A number of writers, however, continued to run this deliberate risk, including Evtushenko, whose work, *A Precocious Autobiography*, raised a hornets' nest in the Soviet Union. The poet was accused in *Komsomolskaya Pravda* of misleading the Union of Writers by showing them a shortened version of his autobiography.[137] (This implies a ruling that works destined for publication abroad must receive prior clearance.)

Nevertheless Evtushenko was too well-known internationally to meet the fate of others, like the poet, philosopher and scientist, A. Esenin-Volpin (the illegitimate son of the famous poet, Esenin) who had had a collection of poems and philosophical essays smuggled out of the Soviet Union and published in the West.[138] The introduction described how he had been arrested and locked up in a psychiatric prison a few weeks after he had gained a Doctorate of Philosophy. Esenin-Volpin said:

'Actually, only a morally and mentally defective person can fail to reach a stage of extreme indignation in the Soviet Union. If this were not so, the Communists would have no reason to seal up their borders.'[139]

The introduction ended with the words:

'There is no freedom of the Press in Russia, but who can say that there is no freedom of thought?'[140]

On December 27, 1962, *Pravda* published a letter by his sisters who wrote that their nephew had 'repeatedly been treated in a psychiatric hospital' and mentioned 'the ravings of a sick man', taking the cue from Ilichev's similar comments a few days earlier.[141]

Also in 1962, a book containing two allegorical stories was published in Britain.[142] The author's pseudonym was Ivan

Valery, but he was a fairly well-known Soviet writer, Valery Tarsis, who was put into a lunatic asylum for sending the manuscripts abroad.*[143] He described his experiences in the *Kanatchikova dacha* (as the Kashchenko Psychiatric Institute in Moscow is popularly known) in an autobiographical novel, *Ward 7*,[144] a title recalling one of Chekhov's most sombre stories, *Ward 6*. The novel describes how 'madmen' are locked up on political and arbitrary grounds and shows that many in this category pass through various mental institutions in Moscow and elsewhere. A sculptor, M. Naritsa, who had sent an auto-biographical novel abroad is known to have met such a fate.[145] Early in 1966 there was news of the arrest of a group of young people in Leningrad for publishing one of the clandestine literary magazines which are a feature of the Soviet cultural scene. The person chiefly responsible apparently received a seven-year sentence.[146] But doubtless these known cases only form the tip of the iceberg.[147] Another punitive measure which the authorities use on occasion is the time-honoured Russian tradition of exile to a remote region.

Before Khrushchev was deposed two more highly political novels were published, both with a bearing on him. *The Difficult Years* appeared at the end of 1963 and the career of its author, N. Sizov, a party official, had links with Khrushchev's own. The work had as its hero a Khrushchev-like figure who, it was implied, stood up to Stalin on agricultural issues and even dared to persist in his own ideas.[148] Thus *The Difficult Years* was an addition to Khrushchev's own considerable 'cult of personality'.

The other novel, *Swiftly Fleeting Days*, had as its villain a figure which from hints scattered about the text, could easily be identified with Khrushchev.[149] It depicted present-day political skulduggery at a high level indeed for a Soviet novel, within the leadership of a fictional Central Asian Republic. The work had a considerable grasp of genuine background detail and of the facts of Soviet political life. The author, N. Virta, had been in the news the same year for his reprehensible personal be-haviour.[150] His novel could be interpreted as an attempt to tear the mask from politics in the Soviet Union, but as so often in Soviet literature, motives remain ambivalent and unexplained.

* Tarsis was in fact allowed to leave the USSR in 1966 and, shortly afterwards, deprived of his Soviet nationality in accordance with a law of 1938 (*Pravda*, February 21, 1966).

Curiously enough, a film showing in Moscow soon after Khrushchev's removal was also interpreted as referring to the former Party leader.[151].

The régime of Brezhnev and Kosygin moved cautiously in the cultural field. Intellectuals were initially encouraged by the firm measures belatedly taken against Lysenko and his supporters and the reinstatement of scientists who had had the thankless task of fighting them and their faking of science. Pleas for an extension of the social sciences in various directions were made, and although strict subordination to Party and State interests was urged, the possibility of interesting developments in the long term did arise.[152] There was a tone of temporising in the first pronouncements on cultural themes which was not dispelled by a more important article, signed by *Pravda's* new editor, Rumyantsev, which appeared on February 21, 1965. Its final section dealt with the arts and sought to give the impression that it was not the Party's task to throw its weight about in cultural affairs. To this effect Rumyantsev quoted Lenin and a 1925 decree aimed against 'amateurish, incompetent administrative interference in literary affairs'.* Yet heavy qualifications were also included: the Party could not passively await the judgment of time on works of art. A reference to the existence of 'various schools and trends, various styles and genres' stipulated that they should be 'united by the unity of a dialectic and materialist outlook and by the unity of the principles of Socialist Realism'.

The suggestion that the Party leaders had not committed themselves to any firm cultural policy was borne out in an unusual exchange between the editors of the two main Soviet newspapers, *Pravda* and *Izvestiya*. In an editorial footnote on August 14, 1965, *Izvestiya* had stigmatised Aksenov, Yashin, some young Leningrad writers and the magazines *Novy Mir* and *Yunost* for favouring 'a negative depiction of contemporary life'. In the course of a turgid article the following month,[153] Rumyantsev took issue with *Izvestiya* and another newspaper for their suggestion that 'the depiction and criticism of the darker side of reality allegedly signifies "savouring" those sides'.[154]

The authorities also made gestures of good intent. Ilichev was removed from the Central Committee Secretariat and

* See p. 33.

transferred to the Ministry of Foreign Affairs.[155] The fate of the Ideological Commission itself was not clear, but there was an unrevealing reference to it in November, 1965.[156] Writers such as Akhmatova, Voznesensky, Evtushenko, who had been out of favour at various times, were allowed to travel abroad again. On the other hand, those who sent manuscripts abroad still fell foul of the authorities.*

The mixture therefore appears to be much the same as before the party's heavy intervention in 1962–63. The two factions show no sign of compromise.[157] The Sinyavsky-Daniel trial did not help to lessen tensions. The postponement of the Writers' Congress (originally due in June, 1966 according to *Pravda* of January 28, 1966) was probably symptomatic.

Probably the party will be reluctant to identify itself too closely with the detested 'retrogrades' once more for fear of protest within and consequences outside the Soviet Union. At the 23rd Congress, for instance, Brezhnev deliberately maintained a balance, repeating that the 'party opposes administrative methods and arbitrary decisions in artistic and literary matters', although he went on immediately to refer to the criteria of party-mindedness and the class approach (*Pravda*, March 30, 1966). Lower-level party leaders and ideologists took a notably harder line, especially with regard to the magazines *Novy Mir* and *Yunost* (the latter published a contrite editorial in its April issue).

There are signs, however, that the Soviet authorities are well aware of the propaganda advantages to be gained from sending certain writers with controversial reputations abroad to represent their country. It is an irony of the Soviet literary scene that the same writers are not popular with a section of uncompromising Soviet intellectuals who contend that if any controversial works achieve publication it is because they perform the function of an official safety-valve. There is some substance in this charge, but it cannot be denied that the debates occasioned even by works which are officially sponsored (*e.g. One Day in the Life of Ivan Denisovich*) are a relatively healthy phenomenon in a society which, for so long, has had artificialities foisted on it under the guise of literature.

* *See* Appendix p. 157.

They touched you up with powder,
They touched you up with rouge!
Your clothes were re-dyed and re-tailored!
You were filled with heart-rending cries
And the puny were raised to giants' estate!
History:
You tramp!
What use is all the dust of your archives then?
Stop lying!

*   *   *   *   *   *   *   *

You will become the most precise of sciences!
You will, you must!
That's what we want.

(From *History*, by Robert Rozhdestvensky).[158]

The post-Second World War campaign against 'bourgeois cosmopolitanism' and 'kowtowing to the West' also redirected the course of Soviet historiography. The official xenophobia then current insisted that historians should emphasise the essential self-sufficiency of the pre- and post-revolutionary Russian States, the Great Russian character of the body politic from the earliest times, the beneficial nature for the non-Russian nationalities of the annexation by Russia of their territories. As regards Soviet relations with Western countries and Western history in general, a more tendentious and exclusively 'patriotic' interpretation was imposed upon Soviet historians. This was shown, perhaps most strikingly, in the development of successive works dealing with war (*see* preamble to this section), and in the vexed question of the Allied intervention after the Bolshevik Revolution. The relatively objective treatment of this theme by historians of the Pokrovsky school in the 1920s was superseded in the next decade by highly tendentious accounts devoted entirely to the predatory anti-Soviet nature of the operation.

In contrast, during the Second World War and in the period immediately following, this topic had been treated much more circumspectly. Now, however, the virulent tone of the 1930s was to be resurrected and, to meet the current needs of Soviet propaganda, the US was for the first time to be portrayed as the leader of the 'anti-Soviet conspiracy'.

The first firm indications of the demands now to be made on

Soviet historians became apparent in March, 1949, when, at meetings held by the Academy of Social Sciences attached to the Central Committee and the Historical Faculty of Moscow University, a number of the most prominent historians were attacked. Authorities on Britain and the US were accused of having become apologists for those countries.[159] In addition, the editorial board of the leading historical journal, *Voprosy Istorii,* was radically reorganised. When the issue for February, 1949, finally appeared in June, nine members of the previous board were no longer listed among the new board of eleven.

The Party now maintained strict surveillance over Soviet historians. Among the many taken to task was the eminent archaeologist, M. I. Artamonov, who was censured in *Pravda* for stating that the Khazar Khanate had served as a pattern for the organisation of the Kievan State, whereas the truth allegedly was that State organisations had existed among the East Slavs long before the Khanate. Artamonov's interpretation was an 'obvious survival of the harmful views of bourgeois historians, who belittled the original nature of the development of the Russian people'.[160] Several other historians were also attacked for overlooking the fact that Slavs inhabited the Crimea at an early date.[161] Another professor, A. N. Berstam, was severely criticised for a 'vicious book' in which he allegedly over-estimated the rôle of the Huns in the overthrow of the Roman Empire and maintained that their culture was superior to that of the Slavs.[162]

The overwhelming majority of the historians attacked in the party Press recanted. Typical was the grovelling 'confession' made by B. Porshnev, who had written a number of works on the feudal era:

'I must confess that I am very late in making my self-criticism—more than two years after my articles were first subjected to criticism. . . . At the present time I am finishing work on a theoretical book on the feudal epoch, which I have tried to write by following in everything, as far as I am capable, the instructions and thoughts of our great leader, J. V. Stalin. I adopted as the basis for this work a study and a profound contemplation of J. V. Stalin's new work of genius. . . .With this book, as with all my future work, I will try to repair the damage I have inflicted on Soviet historical science by my mistakes.'[163]

The model for all works on party history in this period was

Stalin's notorious *History of the All-Union Communist Party: A Short Course*, published in 1938. Not that scholars were eager to come to grips with recent history: between the date of the *Short Course's* publication and Stalin's death in 1953, 'only one doctoral dissertation on party history was defended in the country', according to A. Shapkarin of Moscow University. Similarly, not a single dissertation on party history or Soviet society in general was defended in Georgia in the twenty years after Beriya's book on Transcaucasian Party history appeared in 1935.[164]

In the years following Stalin's death, there were signs of a certain relaxation in the previously rigid ideological controls over Soviet historians.[165] In September, 1954, the Institute of History of the USSR Academy of Sciences, through its journal *Voprosy Istorii*, decried the frequent simplification and embellishment of Soviet history and published a complaint against the MVD's hold over historical archives.[166] A year later, Soviet historians were allowed to participate in an international conference in Rome and reminded that 'historical science cannot exist in isolation in any given country. Acquaintance with the work of foreign historians enriches our own science and enables it to solve important historical questions correctly'.[167]

However, the previous line on how history was to be written remained inviolate in its essentials, *Kommunist* continued to pursue the theme that the historical past of the Russian people was still being belittled and that this 'was bound up with the anti-historical views of the so-called Pokrovsky school, with harmful cosmopolitan theories'.[168] A major work on the war published by the Institute of History in September, 1955, was as virulent in denouncing the Western Powers' responsibility for its outbreak and their subsequent conduct of operations as any of its predecessors. The work gave the Soviet Union the main credit for the collapse of Mussolini's régime[169] and a disproportionate credit for the defeat of Japan. Soviet readers learned that

'The reactionary circles of the USA and Britain were not interested in the total defeat of Japan, intending only to eliminate her as a competitor in world markets.'[170]

A reversion of the post-war line on history finally became inevitable in the face of the de-Stalinisation campaign which followed Khrushchev's secret speech at the 20th Party Congress. An impetus to revision was given by Khrushchev's and Mikoyan's criticisms of the *Short Course* during the congress and their emphasis on the need for a new textbook on party history 'based on historical fact',[171] It was also boosted by the speech of the leading Soviet historian Pankratova who cited, as examples of the detrimental effect of the personality cult on Soviet historiography, the idealisation of the Tsarist past in general and its influence on the writing of the histories of the Soviet non-Russian nationalities.[172] However, no explicit instructions were given to historians, who were left to determine themselves the limits within which this revision could be carried out without violating the presumptive basic tenets of ideology.

The leading part in this work of historical reconnaissance was played by *Voprosy Istorii* and its deputy editor, E. Burdzhalov. In the issue immediately following the 20th Congress, the editorial suggested, *inter alia*, that a more objective portrayal of the Mensheviks (the pre-Revolutionary opponents of the Bolsheviks) should be given, in which they would no longer be depicted as 'accomplices of the Tsarist autocracy'. As regards the Trotskyists and Right-wing deviationists, they had been guilty of 'anti-Leninist activities' but these should no longer 'be regarded in a simplified form as the actions for foreign intelligence services'[173]—the key charge in the purge trials of the late 1930s.

In subsequent issues of *Voprosy Istorii*, questions as diverse as the attitude of the Bolshevik Party leaders to the Provisional Government immediately after the February Revolution,[174] the rôle played by the Caucasian national hero, Shamil, in his fight against Tsarist Russia[175] and that of Ivan the Terrible and his security bodyguard, the *Oprichina*[176]—considered 'progressive' by Stalin[177]—were subjected to re-interpretation, and a more positive evaluation was given to the work of a number of bourgeois historians and thinkers.

However, the growing concern of the party leadership at the 'snowball' effect of de-Stalinisation, first expressed in the increasingly defensive note of successive official appraisals of Stalin, was also to show itself in the field of history. *Voprosy Istorii* was attacked by *Kommunist* only four months after the 20th Congress.[178] It was stated that *Voprosy Istorii's* 'highly dubious formulations' were being 'uncritically accepted' in academic circles.[179] Yet the journal was still able to counter-attack, and characterised a critical article in *Party Life* as being directed at leaving everything as it used to be'.[180]

The events of that autumn in Eastern Europe and consequent campaign against revisionism made it unlikely that these altercations between party organs and a historical journal would be allowed to continue. *Pravda* joined in the attack on the authors of a number of articles in the journal,[181] and the matter was finally resolved by a Party Central Committee decree of March 9, 1957.[182] This charged the journal with distorting history on various sensitive issues, with 'essentially orientating Soviet historians towards a weakening of the struggle against bourgeois ideology in historiography' and with refraining from 'criticism of the revisionist and nationalist articles which have acquired a particularly wide circulation in the Yugoslav Press'. Additional charges were adduced by *Kommunist* in March.

The decree proclaimed that Pankratova, the Chief Editor, was to be severely reprimanded, that Burdzhalov was to be dismissed and that N. Matyushkin, author of works on Soviet patriotism and formerly a leading functionary in the State Publishing House for Political Literature, was to be appointed to the newly created post of First Deputy Editor. Various bodies including *Agitprop* were charged with 'strengthening the staff of the editorial board'. When the May, 1957, issue of *Voprosy Istorii* finally appeared, only four of the original eleven members of the editorial board were among the fifteen members of the new board.[183]

In June, 1959, the official successor to the *Short Course* was published under the title *The History of the CPSU*. The new line it expounded was essentially a modification of *some*, rather than the revision of the *main*, post-war tenets that the 20th congress had seemed to presage. The new textbook, in removing the more obvious traces of the personality cult, divested Stalin of some of the more questionable achievements recorded in the *Short Course*, and, in general, subordinated his personal rôle in events to that of the Party Central Committee. Yet there were few instances of factual revision in relation to his activities. Where allusions were made to Stalin's 'mistakes', references were oblique and fragmentary. For example, the wartime deportation of five Caucasian nationalities, roundly denounced by Khrushchev in his secret speech, was only mentioned in the context of certain vindicatory steps taken by the

Party Central Committee after 1953. Moreover, not only was no specific reference made to the Moscow political trials of the late 1930s, but the main responsibility for acknowledged excesses during the purges was transferred to Ezhov and Beriya.

The Stalinist practice of creating 'unpersons', disgraced leaders subsequently omitted from all official publications, was also followed in the new work. While many former 'unpersons' in the shape of old Bolsheviks were rehabilitated, the names of Khrushchev's defeated opponents, Malenkov, Molotov and Kaganovich, had all but disappeared from the positive side of the record. One of the more striking instances of this was in reference to the wartime State Committee of Defence, of which all three were members. Another example related to the 19th Party Congress, where the main report was given by Malenkov on behalf of the Central Committee.[184] That fact was entirely omitted from the relevant passage which now recorded that

'The 19th Party Congress discussed the report on the changes in the Party Statutes delivered by N. S. Khrushchev.'[185]

It is instructive to compare, in turn, this 1959 history with a 'supplemented' and much revised edition published at the end of 1962. With one minor exception, the editorial board remained the same: the numerous re-evaluations were therefore clearly carried out at the behest of the party. The most sensitive topic is perhaps the rôle of Stalin, and what credit was allowed him in 1959 was now cut down to a minimum.[186] Further derogation of the anti-Party group of Molotov, Kaganovich, Bulganin, etc. took place.[187] Khrushchev's own 'cult of personality' was boosted considerably in the new edition; even a remark made by him when he was 28 years old was resurrected.[188] This was in line with the policy of stressing Khrushchev's achievements, particularly during the war, at the same time as Stalin's were being played down. Amongst the many reappraisals in the field of foreign affairs, complementary references to Mao Tse-tung and Chinese tactics generally were dropped from the 1962 edition.[189]

Meanwhile, intensified efforts had been made to stop historians from devoting themselves to subjects that had no relevance to the present.[190] 'Scholarly Councils' were among the devices introduced at the end of 1950s to co-ordinate and supervise the researches of historians.[191].

Early in 1960, a Central Committee resolution 'On the Tasks of Party Propaganda under Present-Day Conditions' contained a passage which took historians, amongst other scholars, to task for their lack of a 'bold and creative approach to life', for their weak development of 'urgent theoretical and practical questions' and their frequent preoccupation with 'old and barren problems'.[192] Historians were enjoined to produce a multi-volume party history, works on Communist construction, on the Socialist system, the world Communist movement, the crisis of capitalism, the disintegration of the colonial system and the development of the national-liberation struggle of the peoples of Asia, Africa, and Latin America.[193]

In 1960, *Voprosy Istorii* which was intended to be 'the leading central Soviet historical journal' underwent various structural changes which had the aim of making it 'the Party's reliable assistant in the cause of party propaganda and the Communist education of workers'.[194]

The further onslaught on Stalin at the 22nd congress in 1961 meant that the Party's ideological watchdogs, notably Ilichev, were forced to remind historians and other scholars what their true tasks were. That the mood of the latter was often one of cynicism or bewilderment emerged from an important All-Union Conference of Historians held in December, 1962. The frankness of many of the speakers' remarks could not be judged at the time because it was not until 1964 that the conference proceedings were published—in an abbreviated form, at that, and only in an edition of 5,000 copies.[195] It was a sign of the times that Burdzhalov himself spoke at the conference; he was stated to have a post at the Moscow State Pedagogical Institute named after Lenin.[196] In fact what was printed of his speech was courageously polemical: he demonstrated how a prominent historian, Sidorov, had attacked his own ex-teacher (the famous Pokrovsky) although Sidorov was himself one of the 'group of covert and overt enemies of the struggle against the cult of personality after the 20th congress'.[197] Burdzhalov went on to describe how historians had for years been the propagandists of Stalin's works:

'No one makes any reference to them now, the references have simply been crossed out. . . . It is said that certain theses in Stalin's works are correct and others incorrect. But which ones?'[198]

He concluded by calling, like many others,[199] for an end to Stalinist interpretations of history and discreditable methods of moulding it. Defiantly probing old wounds, he stated by way of an example:

'In 1956 there was a discussion in the Institute of History on the question of Shamil; the proceedings were set up in print, but it was decided not to publish them.'[200]

Sidorov had already admitted that in his day he had praised Stalin. He had continued, however, by implicating those now in leading positions who have contrived to forget their own past:

'. . . we have a whole series of other, more prominent historians, such as Academician P. N. Pospelov, for instance, who took up quite specific attitudes. And then when the time for a complete change comes, they say: Yes, we must return to Lenin. Yes, we must. But exemplify this in your actual writing and say a couple of words, at least about your mistakes.'[201]

Indicative of the confusion surrounding the teaching of Soviet history was this question which Pospelov read out during a winding-up speech:

'Students ask whether Bukharin and others were spies for foreign States: what do you advise us to answer?'[202]

The main issue facing historians and others now is: where is the line to be drawn if the party admits that some people were executed and repressed on false charges? Why should the party's current limited reappraisals be taken as the last word? The defensive attitude displayed towards the use of archives by Pospelov and Ponomarev[203] in the face of pressure[204] is significant in this context.

Many speakers dwelt on the party-approved theme of the need to 'unmask' and counter Western 'falsifiers' of Soviet history. Yet the primitive manner in which this is usually carried out was itself the object of derision by a leading historian, M. Kim:

'Is much advantage to be gained from the fact that, for instance, in every dissertation offered for the post-graduate degree of candidate, bourgeois falsifiers are "unmasked" by the author despite his being insufficiently conversant with his opponents' literature, and so frequently having to substitute for scholarly conclusions barbed remarks aimed at two or three authors chosen at random?'[205]

The 1962 conference thus went much further than was probably intended. Party-minded injunctions sounded more than usually hollow when juxtaposed with reports of the hounding of historians in the relatively recent past and of distortions of fact which still occurred.

In 1963 historians were again accused several times of remoteness from life and other familiar charges.[206] The first issue that year of the journal, *Voprosy Istorii KPSS* (established in the aftermath of the 'Burdzhalov affair' in 1957) showed that there had been a radical editorial purge. Only five of the eleven previous members of the board remained and it was expanded to fourteen. Two prominent ideologues, Pospelov and Snastin, became members. The reshuffle occurred after a Central Committee resolution severely critical of the journal was passed the previous November.[207] The party's dilemma emerged clearly from the following injunctions:

'The journal must struggle to liquidate the harmful effects of Stalin's cult of personality in historical and party scholarship. . . . At the same time, the journal is obliged to attack . . . any attempts to undermine the bases of Marxist-Leninist theory under the pretext of the struggle against the cult of the personality and attempts to rehabilitate anti-Marxist views and tendencies which have been crushed by the party.'

A further provision of the same resolution was that it was 'necessary for material about prominent figures in the Communist Party and the Soviet State' to be published.[209] The first person to come to mind in this context would have been Khrushchev. Yet historians were all too aware of where a previous 'cult of personality' had led them and their profession.

Differing interpretations of history had become an issue in Sino-Soviet polemics. Extravagant Chinese claims were derided,[210] for instance, and linked to charges that the Chinese were distorting history for national and even racial reasons. Chinese views on the beneficial effects of the Mongol conquests, for instance, led to sharp rejoinders.[211] It is interesting to note that even archæological discoveries were pressed into service by the Russians some time later to try and prove that cultural influences had gone from West to East, and not *vice versa*. Artefacts several thousand years old were thus used to score points in a contemporary geo-political dispute in which border lands are an important element.[212] Similarly, the publication of 'new' documents by Lenin in recent years often signified more than a mere addition to Leniniana: the documents have been deliberately used to comment on topical issues, such as current Sino-Soviet relations and polemics.[213]

News of more frank comments apparently made at a meeting of historians, held at the Academy of Sciences on June 17–18, 1964, came nearly a year after the event *via* foreign students who had been present.[214] The participants discussed the draft text of the ninth volume of a 12-volume *History of the USSR from the Most Ancient Times [sic] to Our Days*. (The volume in question deals with the crucial 1933–41 period and is known to have gone through 'the stage of revision and extensive discussion by the scholarly public'.[215]) The following highly sensitive points were apparently among those raised with a view to their inclusion or discussion in the volume: some leading party figures had been rehabilitated—but not political prisoners in general; the possibility that the 1939 Nazi-Soviet pact contained several secret clauses, as stated in the West; Soviet participation in the Spanish Civil War; the personality of Kirov's murderer, Nikolaev (and the personality of Stalin himself); the avoidability of shooting Zinoviev and Kamenev, as well as leading Polish Communists during the war; and the allegedly beneficial effects of the 1939 Russo-German partition of Poland. (The last were among points put by A. Snegov, a Party member since 1917, who had also made an outspoken speech at the 1962 conference of historians.)

While other speakers thought that comments had been too critical, a member of the editorial board, Yakubovskaya, conceded:

'We must write in such a way that we need not burn with shame in ten years' time.'

Yet she also argued that the book revealed as much about the Nazi-Soviet pact as 'could or should be said now'. The details of this routine meeting, which leaked out in an arbitrary manner, show how even the most sensitive topics are at last being raised within a closed circle, if not yet in public.[216]

1964 saw the publication of the first volume of another, long-awaited, six-volume party history. Although this dealt with the pre-history of the Bolshevik Party (1883–1903), it became involved in a typical Soviet 'unpersoning' exercise. The victim was now Khrushchev himself, originally mentioned several times in the preface (a preface which was, incidentally, thought worthy of publication in successive issues of *Pravda*[217]). For instance the first printing of the history states:

'Good Communists can be proud of the high evaluation placed on the activity of Comrade N. S. Khrushchev on the day of his glorious 70th birthday by Marxist-Leninist fraternal Parties who noted the rôle of N. S. Khrushchev in the unmasking of the cult of personality, in the creative development of Marxist-Leninist theory and the implementation of great revolutionary transformations.'[218]

Shortly after Khrushchev's downfall in October 1964, a new edition of this volume was produced.[219] It was stated to have been 'signed for printing from the matrices on October 20th, 1964'; all mention of the Soviet leader was deleted. This was doubtless a case of 'subsequent censorship'.

The next stage was to boost the image of the new leaders. A two-volume anthology of historic Party documents, published in the spring of 1965,[220] not only avoided the publication of any speeches by Khrushchev, unlike the previous edition, but worked in two speeches by Brezhnev and one by Kosygin.

History was also revised by having Stalin written back into it, to a certain extent. (The absurdity of euphemistically avoiding his name in the multi-volume *History of the Great Patriotic War* had in fact been pointed out previously to an audience of historians.[221]) Early in 1965 there were signs of a more balanced recognition of Stalin's wartime activities,[222] one implication being that Khrushchev's own wartime rôle would henceforth be relegated to obscurity again. It is not surprising, therefore, that Soviet historians speak of 'specific difficulties'[223] attendant upon the writing of recent history.

As in every intellectual and scholarly field within the Soviet Union at this juncture, there is a gap between the party's dictates and their implementation by all concerned. Academician Ponomarev has defined an historian in these terms:

'An historian is not an impartial narrator who sets down the facts and arranges them, albeit in a scientifically-based scheme. He is a fighter who sees his aim as bringing the history of the past to the service of the struggle for Communism. . . .'[224]

Yet historians have dared to ask some relatively barbed questions in recent years, albeit mainly in private conference. Perhaps this explains why purely party bodies (*e.g.* the Institute of Marxism-Leninism and the Academy of Social Sciences attached to the Central Committee) have concerned themselves increasingly with the teaching of non-party subjects and publication of works on aesthetics, literature, musicology, agrarian history and foreign policy for instance,[225] even though they are ill-equipped to cope with party history itself.[226]

APPENDIX II

From 1959, several works critical of the Soviet way of life were published in the West under the pseudonym of 'Abram Tertz'. The best known of these were a story entitled *The Trial Begins* and an essay on 'Socialist realism'. Satirical stories by 'Nikolai Arzhak' (*e.g. This is Moscow Speaking*, translated in *Dissonant Voices in Soviet Literature*) were also published. Late in 1965, it was rumoured that Andrei Sinyavsky, a senior lecturer at the Institute of World Literature in Moscow, who had contributed to *Novy Mir* and wrote an introduction to the 1965 edition of his friend Pasternak's poems, and Yuly Daniel, a translator mainly of poems from Caucasian languages, had been arrested. *Soviet Russia* of February 11, 1966, stated:

'After measures taken by the Committee of State Security [KGB], it was established that Abram Tertz was Sinyavsky . . . and Nikolai Arzhak his close friend Daniel . . .'.

Their arrest was not, however, announced in the Soviet Press for four months. On January 13, 1966, a lengthy article in *Izvestiya* maligned the two men in Zhdanov-like language, quoting from their works out of context.

The two men were tried under the notorious Article 70 of the RSFSR Criminal Code concerning 'anti-Soviet agitation and propaganda'. They pleaded not guilty and their trial lasted from February 10 to 14, 1966. Although the trial was said to be 'open', attendance was strictly controlled and no foreign journalists (not even from Eastern Europe) were allowed into the court. There were two 'communal prosecutors': one of them, Z. Kedrina, had written another attack on the two accused (*Literary Gazette*, January 22, 1966) while the other, A. Vasilyev, described as having been an 'investigator' in the *Short Literary Encyclopedia*, had himself—by a supreme irony—plagiarised an episode from *The Trial Begins* (*see* letter in *The Guardian*, February 12, 1966). Apparently three senior literary figures, K. Paustovsky among them, had offered their services on behalf of the writers but these had been declined by the authorities (*The Times*, March 16, 1966). The Soviet reports of the trial were heavily slanted. Sinyavsky was sentenced to seven years and Daniel to five years in a 'strict régime corrective labour establishment'.

The partial transcript of the trial which reached the West (*e.g. Sunday Times*, April 17, 1966) showed that despite difficulties put in the way of the defendants, they scored point after point off the prosecutors.

It must have been obvious that the trial and the savage sentences would shock world opinion: protests indeed came from writers all over the world (*e.g. The Times*, January 31 and March 22, 1966); from leading Communists (*e.g. Daily Worker*, February 15, 1966; *L'Humanité* and *L'Unità*, February 16, 1966) and from Soviet intellectuals themselves (*The Times*, March 16; *The Guardian*, March 19, 1966). Nevertheless, groups within the Soviet body politic had considered this show trial expedient in order to warn writers of the limits of criticism. *Pravda* pointed out on February 15, 1966, that 'the sharpest criticism of shortcomings, provided that it serves to uphold our society, to cleanse and strengthen it' was permissible, However:

'Criticism from hostile positions, slanders used to undermine the bases of our social system . . . naturally have been, are being, and will continue to be opposed.'

SOURCES

1. *Spravochnik Sekretarya Pervichnoi Partiinoi Organizatsii*, 1965, p. 4; *Osnovy Politicheskikh Znanii* (Bases of Political Knowledge), State Publishing House of Political Literature, Moscow, 1963, pp. 303–304.

2. For a development of this theme, *see Soviet Literature in the Sixties*, pp. 183f.

3. *Plenum Tsentralnogo Komiteta*, p. 61; *Kommunist*, No. 9, 1963, p. 62.

4. Johnson, pp. 2, 45f; *Soviet Literature in the Sixties*, pp. 93, 97, 194f.

5. Quoted in Counts and Lodge, p. 54.

6. Shestakov, quoted by B. Wolfe in *Problems of Communism*, combined issue Nos. 3 and 4, 1953.

7. *Istoriya SSSR*, Publishing House of Higher Party School and Academy of Social Sciences attached to the Central Committee, CPSU, Moscow, 1963, p. 707; *Istoriya Kommunisticheskoi Partii Sovetskogo Soyuza*, State Publishing House of Political Literature, Moscow, 1962, p. 575.

8. *Istoriya Kommunisticheskoi Partii Sovetskogo Soyuza*, State Publishing House of Political Literature, Moscow, 1959, pp. 567–568.

9. For example, at the inauguration of the Cominform in September, 1947, Zhdanov drew a parallel between the United States and Nazi Germany, both of which, he claimed, were aggressive and anti-Communist. Quoted in Counts and Lodge, pp. 71ff.

10. Swayze, pp. 36f; *Literature and Revolution in Soviet Russia*, pp. 99f.

11. *See*, for instance, Ehrenburg in *Novy Mir*, No. 2, 1965, pp. 50f.

12. *KPSS o Kulture*, pp. 218f.

13. *Ibid.*, pp. 222f.

14. Extracts from the decree and other relevant material were published in *Musical Uproar in Moscow* by A. Werth, Turnstile Press, London, 1949.

15. *Spravochnik Partiinogo Rabotnika*, 1959, pp. 493f.

16. *Bolshevik*, No. 16, 1947, pp. 7f.

17. For instance, 4½ pages were devoted to Stalin in the 1955 edn. of the *Short Philosophical Dictionary* (ed. Rozental and Yudin); in addition, there were individual articles on his theoretical works, *e.g.* 'Marxism and Questions of Linguistics'. The 1963 edn., under the same editors, omitted all items on Stalin and his works: however, it did include an article condemning the 'Cult of Personality'!

18. *Voprosy Filosofii*, No. 3, 1956, pp. 1f.

19. *See*, for instance, *Soviet Studies*, July 1959, p. 66.

20. *Voprosy Filosofii*, No. 2, 1958, pp. 5f; *Marksistskaya i Burzhuaznaya Sotsiologiya Segodnya*, 'Science' publishing House, Moscow, 1964, p. 4; *Survey*, April 1964, pp. 17–18.

21. *Kommunist*, No. 8, 1962, pp. 63f.

22. *Voprosy, Filosofii*, No. 6, 1962, pp. 4f.

23. *Ibid.*, No. 11, 1963, pp. 8,

9. *See* also *Kommunist Ukrainy*, No. 5, 1963, p. 69.

24. *Voprosy Filosofi*, No. 7, 1965, p. 49.

25. *See*, for instance, *Literaturnaya Gazeta*, August 10, 1954. Examples given in *Conquest*, pp. 61f.

26. *Novy Mir*, No. 6, 1956 (article by Simonov); *B.S.E.*, 2nd edn., Vol. 44, p. 492.

27. *Ibid.*, Vol. 20, p. 347.

28. *See*, for instance, *KPSS o Kulture*, pp. 221, 225.

29. Johnson, pp. 97f.

30. *Teatr*, No. 2, 1954.

31. *Literaturnaya Gazeta*, August 17, 1954; *Sovetskaya Kultura*, June 5, 1954.

32. *Znamya*, No. 4, 1954.

33. The main change was Tvardovsky's replacement as editor of *Novy Mir* by Simonov. The former regained the editorship in 1958.

34. *Kommunist*, No. 12, 1955; *Pravda*, November 25, 1955.

35. *See*, for instance, *Pravda*, May 25, 1954.

36. *See*, for instance, *Sovetskaya Kultura*, November 22, 1955; *Komsomolskaya Pravda*, December 13, 1955.

37. *Pravda*, January 5, 1956.

38. *Literaturnaya Gazeta*, January 5, 1956.

39. *Literatura i Zhizn*, November 18, 1959.

40. *Literaturnaya Moskva*, Vol. 2, 1957.

41. *Novy Mir*, No. 12, 1962.

42. *Partiinaya Zhizn*, No. 4, 1954, p. 12.

43. Also known as *The Dodgers* in the translation published by Anthony Blond and Flegon Press, London, 1963.

44. The Leningrad *obkom* stated that it had been 'the most flagrant political mistake' to publish the work: *Leningradskaya Pravda*, May 18, 1963.

45. Reprinted in *Izvestiya*, July 2, 1963; another letter, published in *Sovetskaya Rossiya* on April 13, 1963, attacked Abramov and other 'lovers of refuse' who go 'round and about the dungheap'.

46. *Selskaya Zhizn*, October 7, 1964.

47. *Novy Mir*, No. 1, 1965, p. 7. Another *Novy Mir* writer has described how this Party-inspired process affected him: *Sovetskaya Pechat*, No. 3, 1965, p. 18.

48. *Voprosy Filosofii*, No. 5, 1956; Swayze, pp. 145f.

49. *Pravda* and *Izvestiya*, November 25, 1956; *Sovetskaya Kultura*, December 4, 1956.

50. See *Swayze*, pp. 162f for analyses of these and other heterodox works; pp. 187f for the campaign against them.

51. Khrushchev, pp. 40, 43, 47.

52. *Ibid.*, pp. 44–45.

53. *Ibid.*, p. 47.

54. *Literaturnaya Gazeta*, October 8, 1957; Swayze gives partial translation, p. 197.

55. *Literaturnaya Gazeta*, February 15, 1958, stated that it would be convened in December that year, but it was not opened until May 18, 1959, During his visit to Britain in April, 1959, Sholokhov, when asked to explain the delay, implied that the necessary unanimity had not yet been achieved. See *Manchester Guardian*, April 29, 1959.

56. For instance, Semichastny's comment in *Komsomolskaya Pravda*, October 29, 1958: ' "Therefore if we compare Pasternak to a pig, then we must say that a pig will never do what he has done". (Applause).' Extracts from his report translated in *Conquest*, p. 177.

57. *Pravda*, October 29, 1958.

58. *Pravda*, May 24, 1959 (reprinted in Khrushchev, pp. 74f).

59. *Pravda*, May 19, 1963; Rumyantsev's important leading article in *Pravda*, February 21, 1965, while stressing Party leadership in the arts and sciences, also called for avoidance of administrative interference.

60. For the 1962 manoeuvres when liberals were elected and conservatives blackballed, see *Survey*, January, 1963, pp. 19f; Johnson, pp. 2–3, 13–14, 197–198. Similar events took place in early 1965: *Sunday Times*, January 31, 1965. For an expression of continuing unease at the

leadership of certain unions, *see Kommunist,* No. 3, 1965, p. 24.

61. *Literatura i Zhizn,* September 20, 1959.

62. *Literatura i Zhizn,* September (Markov) and 27 (Starikov), 1961. Ehrenburg took issue with the latter in *Literaturnaya Gazeta,* October 14, 1961. See Evtushenko pp. 120f for the poet's own account of *Baby Yar's* publication.

63. Khrushchev, p. 141.

64. The volumes have been published in translation since 1961 by MacGibbon and Kee, London, under the general title *Men, Years, Life.*

65. Johnson, pp. 122f (referring to criticism on this score by Laktionov, Gerasimov and Ermilov).

66. Johnson, quoting the Ermilov polemic (*Izvestiya,* January 30 and February 6, 1963), p. 129. Also relevant to the general background is a 'Letter from a Russian Writer', *Encounter,* June 1964, pp. 88f.

67. *Pravda,* March 10, 1963, trans. in Johnson, pp. 157–158.

68. Johnson, pp. 11–12, 25; quoting Ermilov and Ilichev, pp. 130, 135–6, 145; quoting Khrushchev, pp. 160f.

69. *Ibid.,* p. 157. In fact, Ehrenburg came very close to arrest. *See,* in particular, *Novy Mir,* No. 2, 1965, pp. 56f.

70. *Encounter,* April, 1963, pp. 35f.

71. *Programma i Ustav KPSS,* p. 220.

72. *Ibid.,* p. 221.

73. *Pravda,* October 29, 1961.

74. *Ibid.,* October 25, 1961.

75. *Ibid.,* October 30, 1961.

76. *Dvadsat Vtoroi S'ezd,* p. 73. A story by Aksenov was translated in *Encounter* for April, 1963.

77. *Izvestiya,* March 24, 1963, quoted a conversation between a Party member and a young man who said '... since the "fathers" had made the mistakes let them now try and teach the young'. The latter went on to point out 'in a venomous voice' that the elder generation had only undertaken the battle against the cult *after Stalin's death.* See also Johnson, pp. 26n, 33, 37.

78. Johnson, p. 26 (and index under 'Fathers and Sons').

79. Especially heavy fire was aimed at K. Ikramov and V. Tendryakov's play, *White Flag.* (See Johnson, pp. 20, 83.) Other playwrights were criticised in the 1964 *B.S.E. Ezhegodnik,* p. 92 and *Sovetskaya Kultura,* November 14, 1963, for instance.

80. Young Soviet writers, of course, number among their ranks persons as conservative (and jealous of the publicity and popularity some of their fellows achieve) as any of the literary 'fathers'. *See,* for instance, the bitter polemic between young critics of

the opposing camps in *Oktyabr*, No. 8, 1962.

81. *Novy Mir*, Nos. 3, 4, 5, 1962.

82. Evtushenko, p. 125. Khrushchev apparently confirmed that he had authorised publication in an unpublished speech: *see* Johnson, p. 5.

83. Translated in Johnson, pp. 93f.

84. Johnson, pp. 46–47.

85. *Ibid.*, pp. 4–5; *B.S.E. Ezhegodnik*, 1963, p. 90; *Izvestiya*, November 6, 1962.

86. Published in translation by Praeger, New York, 1963.

87. Evtushenko, p. 125; Johnson, pp. 5–6; *Soviet Literature in the Sixties*, p. 191.

88. *Pravda*, March 10, 1963; trans. Johnson, p. 156.

89. *Pravda*, May 12, 1963; trans. Johnson, p. 212.

90. A summary of early polemics around Solzhenitsyn is contained in Johnson, pp. 70f, 271f and *passim* (*see* index).

91. *Ibid.*, pp. 2, 45f; *Soviet Literature in the Sixties*, pp. 93, 97, 194f.

92. Johnson, pp. 9–10; (p. 7: the other side was also urging its case).

93. *Leningradskaya Pravda*, March 16, 1963. *See* also *ibid.*, May 18 and July 4, 1963, for the ways in which his diatribe was parried.

94. *Komsomolskaya Pravda*, November 27, 1962.

95. *Pravda*, December 2, 1962.

96. Johnson, pp. 7f. 101f. One of the offending paintings,

Nikonov's 'The Geologists', was reproduced in *Iskusstvo*, No. 7, 1965, p. 26.

97. For some of the rumoured exchanges, *see* Johnson, p. 11.

98. *Sovetskaya Pechat*, No. 4, 1963, pp. 14f.

99. *Ibid.*, p. 15.

100. *Pravda*, December 22, 1962.

101. *Literaturnaya Gazeta*, April 2, 1963 (trans. Johnson, p. 195); *The Times Educational Supplement* had listed Surkov as one of the signatories in a report on March 13, 1963.

102. *Sovetskaya Pechat*, No. 4, 1963, p. 15.

103. *Novy Mir*, Nos. 11 and 12, 1962.

104. Johnson, pp. 53–55, 80, 176–7.

105. A *Kiev Radio* broadcast in April 1963 implied that Nekrasov had defended himself at a meeting of intellectuals and ideologists, stating that he considered his works blameless. Also *see Plenum Tsentralnogo Komiteta*, p. 89.

106. *Ibid.*, pp. 258–259.

107. *Pravda*, March 29, 1963. *See* Johnson, pp. 33f, 202f, for a useful translation of the main 'recantations'.

108. *See*, for instance, the Armenian newspaper *Kommunist*, March 31, 1963; *Pravda Ukrainy*, April 10, 1963.

109. *Izvestiya*, April 10, 1963.

110. Well described by the Latvian ideologue, Voss, in *Sovetskaya Latviya*, July 7, 1963.

111. Johnson, pp. 48–49, trans. pp. 210f.
112. *Literaturnaya Gazeta,* April 2, 1963.
113. *Plenum Tsentralnogo Komiteta,* p. 265.
114. Johnson, pp. 57–58.
115. *Pravda,* June 20, 1963.
116. For the reorganisation of the Moscow Writers' Organisation, for instance, *see Literaturnaya Gazeta,* June 11, 1963 and *Literaturnaya Rossiya,* August 2, 1963; a parallel shake-up in the equivalent artists' body was revealed in *Iskusstvo,* No. 9, 1963.
117. Johnson, p. 53n.
118. *Pravda,* May 26, 1963. The way in which the Soviet citizenry reacts to such officially fostered suspicion was described by the writer Tendryakov who was once reported to the local K.G.B. as an American spy: *Delo,* No. 2, 1965, p. 250 (trans. *The New Leader,* March 29, 1965, p. 28).
119. *Pravda,* September 10, 1964.
120. *Daily Worker,* April 13, 1963.
121. *Pravda,* April 13, 1963.
122. Johnson, pp. 62f.
123. *Ibid.,* pp. 64f.
124. On the relatively recent Soviet discovery of Kafka, *see ibid.,* pp. 83–84.
125. *Literaturnaya Gazeta,* August 13, 1963 (trans. Johnson, pp. 240f).
126. Johnson, pp. 66f.
127. *Izvestiya,* August 18, 1963 (trans. Johnson, pp. 245f).
128. *Literaturnaya Gruziya,* No. 12, 1963. *See* Johnson, pp. 79–80 and footnote.
129. *Ibid.,* pp. 78–79. Evtushenko's comeback was given a most hostile reception in *Oktyabr,* No. 12, 1963, pp. 177–178.
130. *Teatr,* No. 4, 1964.
131. *Ibid.,* No. 10, 1964, p. 82.
132. *Pravda,* June 18, 1965.
133. *Literaturnaya Gazeta,* June 4, 1964, referred to the fact that 'positions of principle', were involved and not just 'a private polemic' between the two critics most involved in the Solzhenitsyn controversy.
134. *See,* for instance, *Pravda,* December 1, 1963 (literary critics and scholars); *Pravda Ukrainy,* April 26, 1964 (literary figures, painters, sculptors); *Sovetskaya Kultura,* May 28, 1964 (musicians).
135. Johnson, pp. 39–40. Also *The Régime and the Intellectuals* (same author), p. xvi.
136. *Osteuropa-Recht,* September 1965, pp. 174–175. According to the new Customs Code (*Vedomosti Verkhovnogo Soveta,* No. 20, 1964, p. 377), the Ministry of Foreign Trade, in agreement with the Ministries of Finance and Communications, has drawn up a list of rules governing international postal communications.
137. *Komsomolskaya Pravda,* March 30, 1963; partial trans. in Johnson, p. 200. *See* also *ibid.,* pp. 27–28, 37f, 39.

138. *A Leaf of Spring*, Thames and Hudson, London, 1962.
139. *Ibid.*, p. 5.
140. *Ibid.*, p. 7.
141. *Pravda*, December 22, 1962.
142. *The Bluebottle*, Collins and Harvill, London, 1962.
143. *Observer*, February 17, 1963; *Il Messagero*, December 22, 1964; *Sunday Telegraph*, April 4, 1965.
144. Published first by *Grany*, No. 57, 1965 and then in trans. by Collins and Harvill in 1965; three episodes serialised in the *Observer*, May 2, 9, 16, 1965.
145. *Observer*, February 3 and 17, 1963, Naritsa's work, *An Unsung Song*, published in *Grany*, No. 48, 1960 (under the pseudonym of M. Narymov). *See* also *Ward 7*, p. 7. and the *Guardian*, April 18, 1963.
146. *Le Monde*, January 4 and 8, 1966.
147. *See* also the *Guardian*, October 6, 1965 for an open letter drawing attention to the incarceration of a student with heterodox views.
148. *Oktyabr*, Nos. 3 and 4, 1964. Extracts in *Nedelya*, February 16–22, 1964.
149. *Don*, 7–9, 1964.
150. *Izvestiya*, July 2, 1964.
151. *The Times*, December 28, 1964.
152. *Pravda*, January 10, 1965 (Burlatsky on political science); *Izvestiya*, October 31 and November 22, 1964; *Trud*, November 12, 1964; *Kommunist*, No. 1, 1965, pp. 9f (sociology). The editorial in *Pravda*, November 5, 1964, emphasised that the social sciences were to be subordinated to the Party, however, and *ibid.*, May 11, 1965, suggested how the Party could make use of sociological research.
153. *Pravda*, September 9, 1965.
154. Yet *Pravda* had published articles on August 11 and 29, 1965, whose tone was very similar to *Izvestiya's* offending footnote. Shortly after his attack, Rumyantsev retired on grounds of ill-health (*Tass* in English, September 22, 1965) and was succeeded as editor by a Deputy Foreign Minister, M. Zimyanin.
155. *Pravda*, March 24 and 27, 1965. This move had been foreshadowed in an allegorical poem by Evtushenko about the chairman of a fish farm who caught even the young fish with his 'impossibly narrow'-meshed net, despite the danger of leaving no fish at all. The poem ended with a demand for the chairman's removal (*Novy Mir*, No. 1, 1965, pp. 94f).
156. *Pravda*, November 31, 1965 (Polikarpov's obituary). It was originally rumoured that P. Demichev, a Central Committee Secretary, had been placed in charge of the Commission, but this has not been officially confirmed. Demichev has, however, spoken on ideological matters but avoided Ilichev's haranguing tone.

157. *Novy Mir*, No. 1, 1965, p. 18. Tvardovsky, at the conclusion of his spirited editorial, which had some sharp things to say about pressures on the arts, looked forward to further polemics in the future.

158. *Dyen Poezii*, 1962. Soviet Writer Publishing House, Moscow, 1962, pp. 93–94; partial and free trans. in *The Times Literary Supplement*, March 22, 1963. *Rozhdestvensky*, born in 1932, is a friend of Evtushenko's.

159. *Voprosy Istorii*, No. 2, 1949, pp. 151f.

160. *Pravda*, December 25, 1951.

161. *Ibid.*, June 4, 1952.

162. *Bolshevik*, No. 11, 1952, p. 72.

163. *Voprosy Istorii*, No. 4, 1953, pp. 141–142.

164. *Vsesoyuznoe Soveshchanie Istorikov*, p. 242.

165. *Russia under Khrushchev*, pp. 470f.

166. *Voprosy Istorii*, No. 9, 1954, pp. 5, 120–121.

167. *Ibid.*, No. 8, 1955, p. 7.

168. *Kommunist*, No. 1, 1955, p. 34.

169. *Ocherki Istorii Velikoi Otechestvennoi Voiny*, 1941–1943, p. 257.

170. *Ibid.*, p. 494.

171. *Pravda*, February 15 and 18, 1956.

172. *Ibid.*, February 22, 1956.

173. *Voprosy Istorii*, No. 3, 1956, pp. 7, 9.

174. *Ibid.*, No. 4, 1956.

175. *Ibid.*, No. 3 and 7, 1956.

176. *Ibid.*, No. 8, 1956.

177. *Vsesoyuznoe Soveshchanie Istorikov*, p. 161 (quoting N. Cherkasov's *Notes of a Soviet Actor*, Moscow, 1953).

178. *Kommunist*, No. 10, 1956, p. 24.

179. *Leningradskaya Pravda*, August 5, 1956.

180. *Voprosy Istorii*, No. 7, 1956, p. 222.

181. *Pravda*, November 20, 1956.

182. *Spravochnik Partiinogo Rabotnika*, 1957, pp. 381–382.

183. For a detailed account of the 'Burdzhalov affair', *see* Fainsod in *Encounter*, March, 1962, pp. 82f.

184. *Pravda*, October 7, 1952.

185. *Istoriya Kommunisticheskoi Partii Sovetskogo Soyuza*, 1959, p. 608.

186. *Compare*, for example, *Istoriya*, 1959 edn., pp. 23, 485, 568, 609, 645 with *Istoriya*, 1962 edn., pp. 241, 506, 585, no equivalent passage, 660.

187. Compare, for example, *Istoriya*, 1959 edn., pp. 155, 384 with *Istoriya*, 1962 edn., pp. 160–161, 404.

188. *Istoriya*, 1962 edn., pp. 220, 540–554, 555, 644, 649.

189. Compare *Istoriya* 1959 edn., p. 453 with *Istoriya* 1962 edn., p. 475.

190. An article in *Soviet Studies* for January, 1965, pp. 255f illustrates this theme in detail.

191. A leading Soviet historian, A. Sidorov, complained of the number of hurdles a

work had to cross before publication now, as opposed to 1924. One of the 'editorial' agencies involved was a Scholarly Council: *Vsesoyuznoe Soveshchanie Istorikov*, p. 333.

192. *Spravochnik Partiinogo Rabotnika*, 1961, p. 491.

193. *Ibid.*, pp. 504–505.

194. *Voprosy Istorii*, No. 8, 1960, pp. 19, 20.

195. *Vsesoyuznoe Soveshchanie Istorikov*, 'Science' Publishing House, Moscow, 1964.

196. *Ibid.*, pp. 367, 517.

197. *Ibid.*, pp. 368, 369.

198. *Ibid.*, p. 369.

199. *See*, for example, *ibid.*, pp. 22, 40, 161, 258, 268–275, 347.

200. *Ibid.*, p. 370.

201. *Ibid.*, pp. 334–335.

202. *Ibid.*, p. 298.

203. *Ibid.*, pp. 296, 502.

204. *Ibid.*, pp. 362, 375, 502.

205. *Ibid.*, p. 389, also pp. 123, 440.

206. *Soviet Studies*, January 1965, pp. 263, 264.

207. *Spravochnik Partiinogo Rabotnika*, 1963, pp. 454f.

208. *Ibid.*, p. 455.

209. *Ibid.*, p. 456.

210. *Voprosy Istorii*, No. 10, 1963, pp. 6f.

211. *Ibid.*, pp. 12f.

212. *The Guardian*, September 3, 1964; *Pravda*, September 4, 1964; *Izvestiya*, September 5, 1964.

213. *See*, for instance, *Pravda*, April 20 and 22, 1964.

214. *The Economist*, May 15, 1965, p. 750; the reference should be to the May issue of the Polish emigré journal, *Kultura* (published in Paris).

215. *Vestnik Akademii Nauk SSSR*, No. 11, 1964, p. 10.

216. *See ibid.*, for more public (if still implied) criticism of party changes of the historical line.

217. *Pravda*, September 21, 22, 23, 1964.

218. *Istoriya Kommunisticheskoi Partii Sovetskogo Soyuza*, Vol. 1 (signed off to the Press on August 27, 1964), p. xlviii.

219. This volume is reviewed in *Survey*, October, 1965, pp. 162f: attention is drawn to the 'sharp practice' it indulges in.

220. *Khrestomatiya po Istorii KPSS* (A Reader on CPSU History). Political Literature Publishing House, Moscow, 1965, pp. 657f.

221. *Vsesoyuznoe Soveshchanie Istorikov*, p. 361.

222. *See*, for example, *The Times*, April 22 and May 11, 1965; *Daily Worker*, April 29, 1965; *The Guardian*, May 11, 1965.

223. *Vestnik Akademii Nauk SSSR*, No. 11, 1964, p. 14.

224. *Vsesoyuznoe Soveshchanie Istorikov*, p. 17.

225. *Soviet Studies*, January, 1965, p. 275n.

226. A Ukrainian historian has declared: 'The Institute of Marxism-Leninism is not regarded as a centre of Party-historical science now because it isn't one.' *Vsesoyuznoe Soveshchanie Istorikov*, pp. 226, 239.

BIBLIOGRAPHY

APN (*Agentstvo Pechati Novosti*), the 'Novosti' (News) Press Agency.

Baku, Kratkaya Adresno-Spravochnaya Kniga (Baku, a Short Address and Information Book), Information Office of the Baku City Executive Committee, 1956.

Barghoorn, F. C.:
 The Soviet Cultural Offensive, Princeton University Press, Princeton, 1960.
 Soviet Foreign Propaganda, Princeton University Press, Princeton, 1964.

Bauer, R. A., *The New Man in Soviet Psychology*, Harvard University Press, Cambridge (Mass.), 1952.

Black, C. E. (ed.), *Rewriting Russian History*, Praeger, New York, 1956.

Boldyrev, N. I. (Compiler), *Direktivy VKP (b) i Postanovleniya Sovetskogo Pravitelstva o Narodnom Obrazovanii* (Directives of the CPSU (b) and Resolutions of the Soviet Government on Popular Education), Vol. 1, Publishing House of the Academy of Pedagogical Sciences of the RSFSR, Moscow-Leningrad, 1947.

Bolshaya Sovetskaya Entsiklopediya, cited as *BSE* (Large Soviet Encyclopedia), 1st edn., 65 vols., with Supplementary vol. on the USSR, Moscow, 1926–47; 2nd edn., 51 vols., with supplementary vol., on the USSR, Moscow, 1949–59. Since then *Ezhegodniki* (yearbooks) have been published.

Bolshevik (Bolshevik), periodical, organ of the Central Committee of the Communist Party of the Soviet Union until November, 1952, when the title was changed to *Kommunist* (Communist).

Boon, J., Eccleshare, C., Barker, R., *The Book Trade in the USSR*. The Publishers Association, London, 1965 (cited as Boon).

British-Soviet Friendship, periodical, organ of the British-Soviet Friendship Society, London.

Brown, E. J., *The Proletarian Episode in Russian Literature*, 1928–32. Columbia University Press, New York, 1953.

Brutskus, B. D., *Economic Planning in Soviet Russia*, Routledge, London, 1935.

Bukharin, N., *Historical Materialism, A System of Sociology*, transl. from 3rd Russian edn., George Allen and Unwin, London, n.d. (1926).

Buzek, A., *How the Communist Press Works*, Pall Mall Press, London and Dunmow, 1964.

Byulleten Verkhovnogo Suda SSSR (Bulletin of the USSR Supreme Court), periodical, organ of the USSR Supreme Court.

Censorship, quarterly, published in London by the Congress for Cultural Freedom.

Conquest, R., *Courage of Genius*, London, 1961.

Counts, G. S., and Lodge, N. P., *The Country of the Blind*, Houghton and Mifflin Co., Boston (Mass.), 1949.

Daily Worker, newspaper, organ of the Communist Party of Great Britain (Renamed *Morning Star*, April 25, 1966.)

Delo (Cause), literary periodical, Belgrade.

Dissonant Voices in Soviet Literature, ed. P. Blake and M. Hayward, George Allen and Unwin, London, 1964.

Dobb, M., *Soviet Economic Development Since* 1917, Routledge and Kegan Paul, London, 1948.

Don (Don), periodical, organ of the RSFSR Union of Writers and its Rostov section (before March, 1965, organ only of the Rostov section).

Dvadsat Vtoroi S'ezd KPSS i Voprosy Ideologicheskoi Raboty (The XXII Congress of the CPSU and Questions of Ideological Work), State Publishing House of Political Literature, Moscow, 1962 (cited as *Dvadsat Vtoroi S'ezd*).

Dvadsaty S'ezd KPSS, Stenografichesky Otchet (XX Congress of the CPSU, a Stenographic Report), 2 vols., State Publishing House of Political Literature, Moscow, 1956.

Ekonomicheskaya Gazeta (Economic Newspaper), weekly, organ of the Central Committee of the Communist Party of the Soviet Union.

Encounter, monthly, London.

Engels, F., *Dialectics of Nature*, Lawrence and Wishart, London, 1941.

Evtikhiev, I. I., and Vlasov, V. A., *Administrativnoe Pravo SSSR* (The Administrative Law of the USSR), Juridical Publishing House of the Ministry of Justice of the USSR, Moscow, 1946.

Evtushenko, E., *A Precocious Autobiography*, Collins and Harvill Press, London, 1963.

Fainsod, M.:
How Russia is Ruled, Harvard University Press, Cambridge (Mass.), 1953.
Smolensk under Soviet Rule, Macmillan, London, 1959.

Fogelevich, L. G. (Compiler), *Osnovnye Direktivy i Zakonodatelstvo o Pechati* (Basic Directives and Legislation on the Press), 6th edn., State Publishing House 'Soviet Legislation', Moscow, 1937.

Grany (Facets), periodical, published by the N.T.S. emigré organisation, Frankfurt/Main.

Gurevich, V., *Kak Delayut Stennye Gazety* (How Wall-Newspapers are Made), State Publishing House of Political Literature, Moscow, 1957.

Hecker, J., *Moscow Dialogues, Discussions on Red Philosophy*, Chapman and Hall, London, 1933.

Ideologicheskaya Rabota Partiinykh Organizatsii (Ideological Work of Party Organisations), Publishing House of the Higher Party School and Academy of Social Sciences attached to the Central Committee of the Communist Party of the Soviet Union, Moscow, 1963.

Il Messagero (*The Messenger*), newspaper, Rome.

Inkeles, A., *Public Opinion in Soviet Russia*, Harvard University Press, Cambridge (Mass.), 1950.

I.P.I. Report, Bulletin of the International Press Institute, Zurich.

Iskusstvo (Art), periodical, organ of the USSR Ministry of Culture, Union of Artists and Academy of Arts.

Istoriya Kommunisticheskoi Partii Sovetskogo Soyuza (History of the Communist Party of the Soviet Union), State Publishing House of Political Literature, Moscow, 1959; 2nd, supplemented edn., 1962.

Istoriya Kommunisticheskoi Partii Sovetskogo Soyuza (History of the Communist Party of the Soviet Union), Volume I of VI vols., two versions, second with altered introduction, Political Literature Publishing House, Moscow, 1964.

Izvestiya (News), newspaper, organ of the Praesidium of the Supreme Soviet of the USSR. (N.B. References are normally to the edn. published the morning after the Moscow evening edn.)

Johnson, P.:
Khrushchev and the Arts: the Politics of Soviet Culture, 1962–64. Manchester Institute of Technology Press, Cambridge (Mass.), 1965 (cited as Johnson).
The Régime and the Intellectuals: A Window on Party Politics. Special Supplement to *Problems of Communism*, No. 4, 1963.

Kazakhstanskaya Pravda (Kazakhstan Truth), newspaper, organ of the Central Committee of the Kazakh Communist Party and of the Supreme Soviet and Council of Ministers of the Kazakh SSR.

Kharkov, Adresno-Spravochnaya Kniga (Kharkov, An Address and Information Book), Kharkov Oblast Publishing House, 1957.

Khrushchev, N.S., *Vysokoe Prizvanie Literatury i Iskusstva* (The Lofty Calling of Literature and Art), '*Pravda*' Publishing House, Moscow, 1963.

Kniga-Issledovaniya, Materialy. Sbornik, IX. (The Book—Researches and Material. A Symposium, Vol. IX of a series.) 'Book' Publishing House, Moscow, 1964.

Kommunist (Communist), periodical, organ of the Central Committee of the Communist Party of the Soviet Union.

Kommunist Sovetskoi Latvii (Communist of Soviet Latvia), periodical, organ of the Central Committee of the Latvian Communist Party.

Komsomolskaya Pravda (Young Communist Truth), newspaper, organ of Central Committee of the Komsomol.

KPSS o Kulture, Prosveshchenii i Nauke (The CPSU on Culture, Education and Science), Political Literature Publishing House, Moscow, 1963.

KPSS v Rezolyutsiyakh i Resheniakh S'ezdov, Konferentsii i Plenumov Ts. K (The CPSU in Resolutions and Decisions of Congresses, Conferences and Plenums of the CC), 7th edition, three volumes, State Publishing House of Political Literature, Moscow, 1954.

Krokodil (Crocodile), periodical, published by *Pravda*.

Kruglak, T. E., *The Two Faces of Tass*, University of Minnesota Press, Minneapolis, 1962.

Kutasov, I., *Naglyadnaya Agitatsiya* (Visual Agitation), State Publishing House of Political Literature, Moscow, 1962.

Le Monde, newspaper, Paris.

Lenin, V. I., *Sochineniya* (Works), 4th edn., 37 vols., Marx-Engels-Lenin Institute, Moscow, 1941–57.

Leningradskaya Pravda (Leningrad Pravda), newspaper, organ of the Leningrad Oblast and City Party Committees and Soviets.

Leninskaya Smena (Lenin's New Guard), newspaper, organ of the Central Committee of the Kazakh Komsomol.

Leontyev, A. and Khmelnitskaya, E., *Ocherki Perekhodnoi Ekonomiki* (Essays on Transitional Economics), The Workers' Publishing House 'Priboi', Leningrad, 1927.

Literatura i Zhizn (Literature and Life), newspaper, organ of the Board of the RSFSR Union of Writers (ceased publication at the end of 1962, replaced by *Literaturnaya Rossiya*).

Literature and Revolution in Soviet Russia, 1917–62, ed. M. Hayward and L. Labedz, Oxford University Press, London, 1963.

Literaturnaya Gazeta (Literary Gazette), newspaper, organ of the Board of the Union of Writers of the USSR.

Literaturnaya Gruziya (Literary Georgia), periodical, organ of the Georgian section of the Union of Writers.

Literaturnaya Moskva (Literary Moscow), 2 vols., ed. by M. Aliger and others, State Publishing House of Artistic Literature, Moscow, 1956.

Literaturnaya Rossiya (Literary Russia), weekly, organ of the Boards of the RSFSR Union of Writers and its Moscow section.

Longo, L. et al., *Problemi e Realtà dell'URSS* (Problems and Reality of the USSR), Editori Riuniti, Rome, 1958.

Manchester Guardian, see *The Guardian*.
Marx, K. and Engels, F.:
   Selected Works in two vols., Lawrence and Wishart, London, 1950 (cited as Marx and Engels).
   Sochineniya (Works), 2nd edn., Vol. 1, State Publishing House of Political Literature, Moscow, 1955.
Molodoi Kommunist (Young Communist), periodical, organ of the Komsomol Central Committee.
Moscow News, weekly, published in Moscow by the Union of Soviet Societies of Friendship and Cultural Relations with Foreign Countries.
Moskva, periodical, organ of the RSFSR Union of Writers and its Moscow section.
Murra, J. V., Hankin, R. M., and Holling, F., *The Soviet Linguistic Controversy*, King's Crown Press, New York, 1951.

Nauchno-Prakticheskii Kommentarii k Ugolovno-Protsessualnomy Kodeksu RSFSR (Scientific and Practical Commentary on the Code of Criminal Procedure of the RSFSR), The State Publishing House of Juridical Literature, Moscow, 1963.
Nedelya (Week), *Izvestiya's* weekly supplement.
New Times, weekly, published by *Trud* (Labour), Moscow.
Novy Mir (New World) periodical, organ of the USSR Union of Writers.

Observer, Sunday newspaper, London.
Ocherki Istorii Velikoi Otechestvennoi Voiny, 1941–45 (Outlines of the History of the Great Fatherland War, 1941–45), Publishing House of the Academy of Sciences, Moscow, 1953.
Oktyabr (October), periodical, organ of the RSFSR Union of Writers.
O Partiinoi i Sovetskoi Pechati, Sbornik Dokumentov (On the Party and Soviet Press, a Collection of Documents), *Pravda* Publishing House, Moscow, 1954.
Organizatsiya Raboty Redaktsii Gazety (The Organisation of Work on a Newspaper's Editorial Board), textbook written by the Higher Party School attached to the CC of the Ukrainian CP, 'Thought' Publishing House, Moscow, 1965.
Osteuropa-Recht (Law in Eastern Europe), quarterly published by the German Society for East European Studies, Stuttgart.

Palgunov, N.G.:
   Tridsat Let: Vospominaniya Zhurnalista i Diplomata (Thirty Years: The Reminiscences of a Journalist and Diplomat), Political Literature Publishing House, Moscow, 1964.

Osnovy Informatsii v. Gazete: Tass i ero Rol (The Bases of Newspaper Information: Tass and its Rôle). Moscow University Publishing House, 1955.

Partiinaya Zhizn (Party Life), periodical, organ of the Central Committee of the Communist Party of the Soviet Union.

Pechat SSSR v 1939 Godu (The USSR Press in 1939), Publishing House of the All-Union Book Shop, Moscow, 1940.

Pechat SSSR v 1961 Godu (The USSR Press in 1961), Publishing House of the All-Union Book Shop, Moscow, 1962.

Pechat SSSR v 1962 Godu (The USSR Press in 1962), Publishing House of the All-Union Book Shop, Moscow, 1963.

Pechat SSSR za Sorok Let (The USSR Press over Forty Years), Publishing House of the All-Union Book Shop, Moscow, 1957.

Philipov, A., *Logic and Dialectic in the Soviet Union*, Research Program of the USSR, New York, 1952.

Plekhanov, G. V., *The Materialist Conception of History*, Foreign Languages Publishing House, Moscow, 1953.

Plenum Tsentralnogo Komiteta Kommunisticheskoi Partii Sovetskogo Soyuza, 18–21 Iyunya 1963. (The Plenum of the Central Committee of the Communist Party of the Soviet Union, 18–21 June, 1963.) A Stenographic Report. Political Literature Publishing House, Moscow, 1964 (cited as *Plenum Tsentralnogo Komiteta*).

Pokrovsky, M. N., *Brief History of Russia*, Vol. 1, Martin Lawrence, London, 1933.

Politicheskoe Samoobrazovanie (Political Self-Education), periodical, organ of the Central Committee of the Communist Party of the Soviet Union.

Pravda (Truth), newspaper, organ of the Central Committee of the Communist Party of the Soviet Union.

Preiskurant na Sovetskie Gazety i Zhurnaly (Price List for Soviet Newspapers and Magazines), 'Soyuzpechat', Moscow, 1964.

Preiskurant na Zarubezhnye Gazety i Zhurnaly (Price List for Foreign Newspapers and Magazines), 'Soyuzpechat', Moscow, 1964.

Preobrazhensky, E. A., *Novaya Ekonomika* (The New Economics), Publishing House of the Communist Academy, Moscow, 1926.

Problems of Communism, periodical, United States Information Agency, Washington (D.C.).

Programma i Ustav KPSS (The Programme and Statutes of the CPSU), Political Literature Publishing House, Moscow, 1962.

Rozental, M. and Yudin, P. (eds.):
Kratky Filosofsky Slovar (Short Philosophical Dictionary), 4th edn., State Publishing House of Political Literature, Moscow, 1955.

Kratky Filosofsky Slovar (Short Philosophical Dictionary), new edn., Publishing House of Political Literature, Moscow, 1963 (cited as Rozental and Yudin).

RSFSR Laws 1917–38; *Sobranie Uzakonenii i Rasporyazhenii Raboche-Krestyanskogo Pravitelstva Rossiiskoi Sovetskoi Federativnoi Sotsialisticheskoi Respubliki* (Collection of Statutes and Orders of the Worker-Peasant Government of the Russian Soviet Federative Socialist Republic), People's Commissariat of Justice of the RSFSR, Moscow.

Russia under Khrushchev: an Anthology from Problems of Communism. Ed. A. Brumberg, Praeger, New York, 1962.

Sovetskaya Belorussiya (Soviet Belorussia), organ of the Central Committee of the Belorussian Communist Party and the Belorussian Supreme Soviet and Council of Ministers.

Sovetskaya Kultura (Soviet Culture), newspaper, organ of the Ministry of Culture of the USSR and the Central Committee of the Cultural Workers' Trade Union.

Sovetskaya Latviya (Soviet Latvia), newspaper, organ of the Central Committee of the Latvian Communist Party and the Latvian Supreme Soviet and Council of Ministers.

Sovetskaya Pechat (Soviet Press), periodical, organ of the USSR Union of Journalists.

Sovetskaya Pechat v Dokumentakh (The Soviet Press in Documents), State Publishing House of Political Literature, Moscow, 1961.

Sovetskaya Pechat v Tsifrakh (The Soviet Press in Figures), Publishing House of the All-Union Book Shop, Moscow, 1948.

Sovetskaya Rossiya (Soviet Russia), newspaper, organ of the Central Committee, CPSU (from April 9, 1966).

Sovetskoe Gosudarstvo i Pravo (Soviet State and Law), periodical, organ of the Institute of State and Law of the USSR Academy of Sciences.

Soviet Literature in the Sixties. An International Symposium ed. by M. Hayward and E. Crowley, Methuen, London, 1965.

Soviet News, newspaper, published by the Soviet Embassy's Press Department in London.

Soviet Studies, periodical, ed. at the University of Glasgow.

Spravochnik dlya Postupayushchikh v Moskovsky Universitet (Handbook for Entrants to Moscow University), Moscow University Publishing House, 1965.

Spravochnik dlya Postupayushchikh v Vysshie Uchebnye Zavedeniya SSSR (Handbook for Entrants to Higher Educational Establishments of the USSR), 'Higher School' Publishing House, Moscow, 1965.

Spravochnik Partiinogo Rabotnika (Party Worker's Handbook), State Publishing House of Political Literature, Moscow, 1957, 1959, 1961, 1963, 1964 (the last issued by the Publishing House of Political Literature).

Spravochnik Sekretarya Pervichnoi Partiinoi Organizatsii (Handbook for the Secretary of a Primary Party Organisation), State Publishing House of Political Literature, Moscow, 1960.

Spravochnik Sekretarya Pervichnoi Partiinoi Organizatsii (Handbook for the Secretary of a Primary Party Organisation), Publishing House of Political Literature, Moscow, 1965.

Spravochnik Zhurnalista (The Journalist's Handbook), 2nd revised and enlarged edn., Leningrad Publishing House, Leningrad 1965.

Stalin, J., *Problems of Leninism*, transl. from the 11th Russian edn., Foreign Languages Publishing House, Moscow, 1953.

Struve, G., *Soviet Russian Literature*, 1917–50, University of Oklahoma Press, Norman (Oklahoma), 1951.

Studenikin, S. S., Vlasov, V. A. and Evtikhiev, I. I., *Sovetskoe Administrativnoe Pravo* (Soviet Administrative Law), State Publishing House of Juridical Literature, Moscow, 1953.

Sunday Telegraph, newspaper, London.

Sunday Times, newspaper, London.

Survey, a journal of Soviet and East European Studies, London.

Tass (Telegrafno Agentstvo Sovetskogo Soyuza), Telegraph Agency of the Soviet Union.

Teatr, periodical, organ of the USSR Union of Writers and Ministry of Culture.

Teatralnaya Entsiklopediya (Theatrical Encyclopedia), 'Soviet Encyclopedia' Publishing House, Moscow. First three vols. published 1961–64.

The Economist, weekly, London.

The Guardian, newspaper, London and Manchester (formerly *Manchester Guardian*).

The New Leader, periodical published for the American Labor Conference on International Affairs, New York.

The Times, newspaper, London.

The Times Educational Supplement, weekly, London.

The Times Literary Supplement, weekly, London.

Timofeev, L. I. and Dementev, A. G. (eds.) *Russkaya Sovetskaya Literatura* (Russian Soviet Literature, 2nd edn.), State Pedagogical Publishing House of the Ministry of Education of the RSFSR, Moscow, 1958.

Tsifry o Pechati SSSR (Figures on the Press of the USSR), Moscow, 1940.

Turkmenskaya Iskra (Turkmenian Spark), newspaper, organ of the Central Committee of the Turkmenian Communist Party and of the Supreme Soviet and Council of Ministers of the Turkmenian SSR.

Ugolovny Kodeks RSFSR (Criminal Code of the RSFSR), State Publishing House of Juridical Literature, Moscow, 1953. (A revised Code has been published since.)

U.S. News and World Report, weekly, U.S. News Publishing Corporation, Washington, D.C.

USSR Laws:

1924–38, *Sobranie Zakonov i Rasporyazhenii Raboche-Krestyanskogo Pravitelstva Soyuza Sovetskikh Sotsialisticheskikh Respublik* (Collection of Laws and Orders of the Worker-Peasant Government of the Union of Soviet Socialist Republics), Administration of Affairs of the Council of People's Commissars of the USSR, Moscow, 1938.

Sobranie Postanovlenii Rasporyazhenii Pravitelstva Soyuza Sovetskikh Sotsialisticheskikh Respublik (Collection of Decrees and Orders of the Government of the Union of Soviet Socialist Republics), Administration of Affairs of the Council of People's Commissars (Council of Ministers from April 1946) of the USSR, Moscow.

Varga, E. S., *Osnovnye Voprosy Ekonomiki i Politiki Imperializma* (Fundamental Questions of the Economics and Politics of Imperialism), State Publishing House of Political Literature, Moscow, 1953.

Vechernyaya Moskva (Evening Moscow), newspaper, organ of the Moscow City Committee of the CPSU and of the Moscow City Soviet.

Vedomosti Verkhovnogo Soveta RSFSR (Gazette of the RSFSR Supreme Soviet), periodical, organ of the RSFSR Supreme Soviet.

Vedomosti Verkhovnogo Soveta SSSR (Gazette of the USSR Supreme Soviet, periodical, organ of the USSR Supreme Soviet.

Vestnik Akademii Nauk SSSR (Gazette of the USSR Academy of Sciences), periodical, organ of the USSR Academy of Sciences.

Vestnik Moskovskogo Universiteta (Herald of Moscow University), periodical published in various series by Moscow University.

Voprosy Ekonomiki (Questions of Economics), periodical, organ of the Institute of Economics of the USSR Academy of Sciences.

Voprosy Filosofii (Questions of Philosophy), periodical, organ of the Institute of Philosophy of the USSR Academy of Sciences.

Voprosy Istorii (Questions of History), periodical, organ of the Institute of History of the USSR Academy of Sciences.

Voprosy Istorii KPSS (Questions of History of the CPSU), periodical, organ of the Institute of Marxism-Leninism attached to the Central Committee of the Communist Party of the Soviet Union.

Voprosy Literatury (Questions of Literature), periodical, organ of the USSR Union of Writers and the Gorky Institute of World Literature of the USSR Academy of Sciences.

Voznesensky, N., *Voennaya Ekonomika SSSR v Period Otechestven-noi Voiny* (The War Economy of the USSR during the Father-land War), State Publishing House of Political Literature, Moscow, 1948.

Vsesoyuznoe Soveshchanie Istorikov (All-Union Conference of His-torians), 'Science' Publishing House, Moscow, 1964.

World Communications: Press, Radio; Television, Film. UNESCO, Paris, 1964.

Yakovlev, I., *Chto Nuzhno Znat Redkollegii Stennoi Gazety* (What the Editorial Board of a Wall Newspaper Needs to Know), State Publishing House of Political Literature, Moscow, 1957.

Yevtushenko, S., *see* Evtushenko.

Zaidel, G. and Tsvibak, M., *Klassovy Vrag Na Istoricheskom Fronte* (The Class Enemy on the Historical Front), State Socio-Eco-nomic Publishing House, Moscow-Leningrad, 1931.

Za Rubezhom (Abroad), weekly, published by the USSR Union of Journalists.

Zarya Vostoka (Dawn of the East), newspaper, organ of the Central Committee of the Georgian Communist Party and of the Geor-gian Supreme Soviet and Council of Ministers.

Zenkovsky, V. V., *History of Russian Philosophy*, two vols., Rout-ledge and Kegan Paul, London.

Zhurnal Moskovskoi Patriarkhii (Journal of the Moscow Patriarch-ate), periodical, published by the Moscow Patriarchate.

Znamya (Banner), periodical, organ of the USSR Union of Writers.

Zvezda (Star), periodical, organ of the USSR Union of Writers.

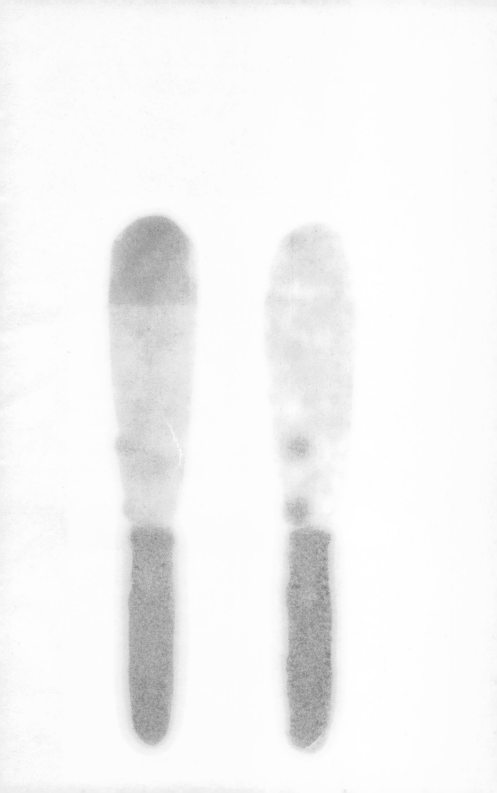

DATE DUE

APR 2 0 1999	